Diabetic Air Fryer Cookbook

Over 100 Healthy & Delicious Low-Carb, Low-Sugar Recipes for Type 1 & Type 2 Diabetes.

30-Day Meal Plan for Beginners Included

Monica Fisher

Legal Notice:
Copyright 2024 by Monica Fisher - All rights reserved.

This document is geared towards providing exact and reliable information regarding the topic and issue covered. The publication is sold on the idea that the publisher is not required to render accounting, officially permitted, or otherwise, qualified services. If advice is necessary, legal, or professional, a practiced individual in the profession should be ordered. From a Declaration of Principles which was accepted and approved equally by a Committee of the American Bar Association and a Committee of Publishers and Associations.

Disclaimer Notice:
The information herein is offered for informational purposes solely and is universal as so. The presentation of the information is without a contract or any type of guaranteed assurance. Readers acknowledge that the author is not engaging in the rendering of legal, financial, medical, or professional advice. Please consult a licensed professional before attempting any techniques outlined in this book. The trademarks that are used are without any consent, and the publication of the trademark is without permission or backing by the trademark owner. All trademarks and brands within this book are for clarifying purposes only and are owned by the owners themselves, not affiliated with this document.

Table of Contents

Introduction 8
   Tips and Tricks 10
Understanding Diabetes 13
   What is Diabetes? 13
   Differences Between Type 1 and Type 2 Diabetes 13
      Type 1 Diabetes 13
      Type 2 Diabetes 14
   The Importance of Diet in Managing Diabetes 14
      Blood sugar control 14
      Weight Management 14
      Nutritional Balance 15
      Meal Timing and Frequency 15
      Individualised Plans 15
   Key Nutritional Considerations for Diabetics 16
      Carbohydrate Management 16
      Fiber 17
      Vitamins and minerals 17
      Hydration 17
      Meal Timing and Frequency 17
      Individualized Plans 18
   The Benefits of Air Frying for Diabetics 18
      Reduced Oil Consumption 18
      Better Blood Sugar Control 18
      Retained Nutrient Content 19
      Enhanced Flavour and Texture 19
      Convenience and Safety 19
      Reduced Formation of Harmful Compounds 20
      Environmental and Economic Benefits 20
      Supporting a Balanced Diet 20
Getting Started with Your Air Fryer 21
   Why Choose an Air Fryer? 21
   Air Fryer Basics: How It Works 23
   The Core Technology: Rapid Air Circulation 23

- Key Components of an Air Fryer 23
- Operating an Air Fryer: Step-by-Step Guide 24
- Maintenance and Cleaning 25
- Essential Tips for Air Frying 26
- Cleaning and Maintenance of Your Air Fryer 28
- Low-Carb, Low-Sugar Cooking: The Fundamentals 31
  - Understanding Carbohydrates and Sugars 31
    - Types of Carbohydrates 31
  - Key Principles of Low-Carb, Low-Sugar Cooking 31
  - Practical Tips for Low-Carb, Low-Sugar Cooking 32
  - Creating Balanced Meals 33
  - How to Modify Recipes for Diabetic Needs 34
  - Understanding the Basics 34
    - Substituting Ingredients 35
  - Cooking Techniques 35
  - Adapting Specific Recipes 36
  - Monitoring and Adjusting 37
  - Practical Examples 37
- Portion Control and Meal Planning 38
  - Portion Control 38
  - Meal Planning 38
  - Adjusting Meal Plans 39
- Stocking Your Pantry with Diabetic-Friendly Ingredients 40
  - Whole Grains and Legumes 40
  - 1. Whole Grains 40
  - 2. Legumes 40
  - 3. Healthy Fats 41
  - 4. Proteins 41
  - 5. Dairy and Alternatives 42
  - 6. Vegetables and Fruits 42
  - Baking Essentials 43
  - Ready-to-Eat Snacks 43

Breakfast Recipes 44
- Air-Fried Veggie Frittata 45
- Almond Flour Pancakes 45
- Air-Fried Avocado Toast 46

4

Air-Fried Breakfast Sausage 46

Air-Fried Greek Yogurt and Berry Parfait 47

Air-Fried Omelette Muffins 47

Air-Fried Tofu Scramble 48

Air-Fried Eggplant and Tomato Breakfast Bake 48

Air-Fried Spinach and Feta Breakfast Wrap 49

Air-Fried Cottage Cheese and Berry Bowl 49

Air-Fried Sweet Potato Hash 50

Air-Fried Mushroom and Cheese Breakfast Bake 50

Air-Fried Zucchini and Egg Breakfast Boats 51

Air-fried Cauliflower Breakfast Bites 51

Air-Fried Breakfast Burrito 52

Air-Fried Spinach and Mushroom Quiche 52

Air-Fried Broccoli and Cheddar Breakfast Cups 53

Air-Fried Apple Cinnamon Breakfast Bites 53

Air-Fried Kale and Egg Breakfast Cups 54

Air-Fried Tomato and Basil Breakfast Tart 54

Lunch Recipes 55

Air-Fried Chicken Caesar Wrap 56

Air-Fried Shrimp Tacos 56

Air-Fried Falafel wraps 57

Air-Fried Turkey and Avocado Sandwich 57

Air-Fried Veggie Quesadillas 58

Air-Fried Chicken and Veggie Skewers 58

Air-Fried Salmon Patties 59

Air-Fried Veggie Spring Rolls 59

Air-Fried Chicken and Black Bean Tostadas 60

Air-Fried Greek Chicken Wrap 60

Air-Fried Zucchini and Mushroom Panini 61

Air-Fried Tuna and Avocado Salad 61

Air-Fried Chickpea and Spinach Wrap 62

Air-Fried Caprese Sandwich 62

Air-Fried Veggie Burger 63

Air-Fried Chicken and Veggie Wrap 63

Air-Fried Spinach and Feta Stuffed Peppers 64

Air-Fried Chicken and Avocado Salad 64

Air-Fried Eggplant Parmesan Sandwich 65

Air-Fried Chickpea and Quinoa Salad 65

Dinner Recipes 66

Air-Fried Lemon Garlic Salmon 67

Air-Fried Chicken and Broccoli Stir-Fry 67

Air-Fried Shrimp Scampi 68

Air-Fried Turkey Meatballs 68

Air-Fried Stuffed Bell Peppers 69

Air-Fried Tofu Stir-Fry 69

Air-Fried Beef and Vegetable Skewers 70

Air-Fried Chicken Parmesan 70

Air-Fried BBQ Pork Chops 71

Air-Fried Vegetable Lasagna Rolls 71

Air-Fried Cajun Shrimp and Vegetables 72

Air-Fried Stuffed Chicken Breasts 72

Air-Fried Greek Chicken and Vegetables 73

Air-Fried Teriyaki Salmon 73

Air-Fried Chicken Fajitas 74

Air-Fried Garlic Butter Shrimp 74

Air-Fried Eggplant Parmesan 75

Air-Fried Lemon Herb Chicken Thighs 75

Air-Fried Coconut Shrimp 76

Air-Fried Zucchini Boats 76

Snacks and Appetizers 77

Air-Fried Zucchini Chips 78

Air-Fried Cauliflower Bites 78

Air-Fried Avocado Fries 79

Air-Fried Mozzarella Sticks 79

Air-Fried Sweet Potato Fries 80

Air-Fried Chicken Wings 80

Air-Fried Jalapeño Poppers 81

Air-Fried Spinach and Feta Balls 81

Air-Fried Stuffed Mushrooms 82

Air-Fried Tofu Bites 82

Air-Fried Falafel 83

Air-Fried Cheese and Broccoli Bites 83

Air-Fried Coconut Chicken Bites ... 84
Air-Fried Garlic Parmesan Asparagus ... 84
Air-Fried Eggplant Fries ... 85
Air-Fried Buffalo Cauliflower Bites ... 85
Air-Fried Chickpea Snacks ... 86
Air-Fried Portobello Mushroom Fries ... 86
Air-Fried Brussels Sprouts ... 87
Air-Fried Onion Rings ... 87

Dessert Recipes ... 88
Air-Fried Apple Cinnamon Rings ... 89
Air-Fried Banana Fritters ... 89
Air-Fried Chocolate Avocado Brownies ... 90
Air-Fried Cinnamon Sweet Potato Bites ... 90
Air-Fried Berry Crumble ... 91
Air-Fried Peach Cobbler ... 91
Air-Fried Blueberry Muffins ... 92
Air-Fried Pineapple Rings ... 92
Air-Fried Chocolate Chip Cookies ... 93
Air-Fried Stuffed Dates ... 93
Air-Fried Lemon Bars ... 94
Air-Fried Raspberry Cheesecake Bites ... 94
Air-Fried Coconut Macaroons ... 95
Air-Fried Pear Chips ... 95
Air-Fried Chocolate-Dipped Strawberries ... 96
Air-Fried Pumpkin Spice Donuts ... 96
Air-Fried Chocolate Zucchini Bread ... 97
Air-Fried Mango Coconut Balls ... 97
Air-Fried Churro Bites ... 98
Air-Fried Apple Cinnamon Rolls ... 98

30 Days Meal Plan ... 99
Conclusion ... 102

Introduction

Managing diabetes through diet is an important part of staying healthy and well. This book aims to present you with a range of tasty, wholesome meals that will make diabetic management easier, more fun-filled, and sustainable. It addresses the needs of people suffering from type 1 and type 2 diabetes by providing over one hundred nutritious and delicious low-carb/low-sugar doctor-approved recipes.

This book is a comprehensive guide with a thirty-day meal plan for beginners aimed at helping you change your eating habits and improve your health. Diabetes changes how the body processes sugar (glucose), which is essential since it fuels most cells in the body and is used by the brain as its primary energy source. But whatever causes your diabetes in particular, it always results in high blood sugar. This condition can lead to serious health problems no matter what kind of diabetes you have. Type 1 diabetes is an autoimmune disorder where the immune system destroys insulin-producing cells in the pancreas. This means that people suffering from type 1 diabetes must use insulin injections to survive. On the other hand, type 2 diabetes has more cases and often happens due to lifestyle factors such as overweight or sedentary living. However, in such cases, the body becomes insulin resistant or does not secrete enough for all functions necessary for the body's life.

The importance of managing diabetes through diet cannot be emphasised enough. Thus, eating a balanced diet helps keep blood glucose levels stable within normal limits, thereby preventing complications associated with diabetes mellitus. To do so requires choosing foods low in sugar and carbohydrates yet rich in Fiber, balanced with good fats and proteins, making managing your Diabetes possible while giving a boost to overall health.

Maybe you are asking where the air fryer comes into play when preparing food.

An air fryer is an innovative kitchen device that uses hot air to fry food. When the air fryer is in use, a fan circulates the heat at a high speed, cooking the food and giving it a crispy layer like frying but with much less oil. It can be regarded as one of the best kitchen devices for preparing diabetic meals that have low-fat content and calorie counts but still taste good.

An air fryer is particularly helpful to people with diabetes since cooking such foods often contains high amounts of fats and calories. By reducing the amount of oil used in cooking, you can reduce the total calorie and fat count in your diet; thus, you can maintain a healthy weight and control your blood sugar levels. Moreover, an air fryer has endless possibilities in terms of the kinds of meals you can make using it – from starters and snacks to main dishes and desserts alike.

There are various reasons why an air fryer is a great addition to any kitchen, particularly for those with diabetes:

- Air fryers use less oil than traditional frying methods, which means they have less fat and calories. This can aid in maintaining healthy body weight and reduce the risk of heart disease, which are among the key things to watch out for in people with diabetes.

- Air fryers can cook various foods, from vegetables and meat to snacks and desserts. This makes it easy to make many diabetic-friendly meals that taste good and are nutritious.

- Air fryers are convenient to use and require minimal preparation time. They also cook food quickly and uniformly, making them ideal for busy people who want to eat healthily but don't have much time for cooking.

- Despite using reduced oil, air fryers produce crispy exteriors and tender interiors, just like traditional frying methods. Hence, you can still enjoy the taste of fried foods without worrying about extra fats or calories.

Before we start on recipes, you must understand how to effectively use your air fryer.

- Every air fryer is slightly different, so read your appliance's manual when it arrives. This will give you important details about operating and maintaining your air fryer.

- Preheating an air fryer ensures it is heated properly before cooking at your desired temperature. This uniformity helps food cook evenly while ensuring its outside becomes crispy. Most preheat times last approximately 3–5 minutes on most models.

- Although air fryers use less oil than conventional frying techniques, adding a small quantity of oil may help achieve crispiness. Spray a little bit of it for the desired results only.

- To ensure even cooking of everything in an air-fryer tray, do not overcrowd the basket. Spread out the food items so hot air passes through each piece separately.

- Shaking the basket or flipping halfway through the cooking process can yield better results for foods prone to sticking or requiring even cooking on all sides.

- Cooking times and temperatures differ depending on the type of food being cooked. Thus, it's advisable to monitor your food and make necessary changes. Most air fryer recipes contain specific directions regarding cooking time and temperature.

Tips and Tricks

- A nonstick cooking spray can prevent food from sticking to the basket and improve its browning and crispiness.

- The slight dryness sometimes experienced when air-frying instead of deep-frying can be mitigated by seasoning your food more heavily with herbs, spices, and marinades to enhance flavour.

- A sheet of parchment paper at the bottom of your air fryer basket prevents sticking and makes cleaning easier. However, remember to leave some space around all edges so that hot air circulates properly.

- Don't hesitate to experiment with various meals using an air fryer. You can try new dishes, including vegetables, meats, fruits and baked goods.

- Monitoring your food while cooking will prevent it from overcooking or burning. Some foods may take longer than others; therefore, you need to check on them regularly to get the desired results.

- Getting it right with air frying can be a bit tricky. Don't lose heart if your initial few trials fail to give you what you want. You'll become more comfortable and confident using your air fryer through time and experience.

- Diabetes management through diet involves portion control and meal planning. Eating the right amounts of food is important to maintain steady blood sugar levels and prevent overeating, which leads to weight gain and other health problems.

- Managing diabetes includes paying attention to portion sizes. To take charge of what gets inside your body and eat a balanced diet without overindulging in food portions, try using smaller plates, weighing your meals or learning how not to eat more than once. The recipes in this book provide proper serving suggestions that will help you stay on track.

- Meal planning helps us make healthier choices instead of making last-minute decisions that may not adhere to our dietary goals. The 30-Day Meal Plan provided in this book is meant to assist you in mapping out meals effectively by providing different options for nutritious dishes tailored towards diabetic patients.

Grocery shopping is therefore necessary to have a well-stocked pantry full of diabetic-friendly ingredients for easy preparation of healthy meals and snacks.

The following are some core ingredients that should always be available:

1. Choose lean proteins such as chicken, turkey, fish, tofu and legumes. These protein sources help stabilize blood sugar levels while keeping you satiated.

2. Choose excellent sources of carbs, such as whole-grain bread or cereals, brown rice, quinoa, etc., which are rich in Fibre and hence energy-giving without causing blood sugar spikes.

3. Healthy fats, particularly those found in avocados, nuts, seeds, olives, and cocoa, promote heart health while increasing satiety.

4. Fantastic vitamin sources include greens, vegetables like broccoli, cauliflower, bell peppers, zucchini, etc., and non-starchy.

5. Berries, apple pears, and citrus fruits have less sugar but highly nutritious antioxidants.

6. If you want to enjoy the sweet taste of Stevia, Monk fruit and Erythritol without affecting your blood glucose levels, use them as a substitute for sugar in recipes.

7. Spices and Herbs: A wide range of spices and herbs should be stocked to add flavour to your meals without using added sugars or unhealthy fats.

8. Almond flour, coconut flour, and flaxseed meal are perfect substitutes for traditional flours that help reduce the amount of carbohydrates used in baking and cooking.

9. With such ingredients in your pantry, you will be better able to prepare nutritious and delicious meals that support diabetes management.

10. With the thirty-day menu, this book can make consuming tasty diabetic-friendly dishes every day an enjoyable task.

Diabetes management is not just about eating; it involves embracing a healthy lifestyle change by being physically active regularly, getting enough sleep, managing stress, and regularly attending medical checkups.

Physical Activity: Regular exercise helps regulate blood sugar levels, improve insulin sensitivity, and support cardiovascular health. In addition to strength training exercises, aim for at least 150 minutes of moderate-intensity aerobic activity each week.

Adequate Sleep: Sufficient sleep is vital for good health and may impact blood glucose levels. Ensure you get between 7 and 9 hours of quality sleep per night.

Stress Management: Chronic stress can interfere with blood sugar levels and overall health. You can manage your stress by practising mindfulness, meditation or breathing exercises.

Regular Check-Ups: It is important to visit your healthcare provider regularly to monitor your diabetes management and general health. Follow the medical practitioner's recommendations for screenings, medications, and lifestyle changes.

Integrating these components into your daily routine can help you develop a holistic approach to managing diabetes and improve your overall sense of wellness.

This book is more than just recipes. It contains everything you need to know about managing diabetes through healthy yet delicious meals that are easy to prepare. By incorporating the principles outlined in this book and using its recipes, you can take charge of what you eat, boost your well-being and enjoy preparing and eating nutritious food.

Remember, diabetes management is a lifelong journey that requires dedication, knowledge and support. This cookbook provides all you need to make healthy eating a sustainable and enjoyable part of your life. We hope that this book will inspire you to try new flavors and experience different cooking styles when using an air fryer.

Thank you for choosing this book as a guide for diabetic-friendly cooking. Good luck with improving your health! I can't wait to see the scrumptious dishes you will create during this journey.

Understanding Diabetes

What is Diabetes?

Diabetes is a chronic illness resulting from inadequate regulation of blood sugar levels by the body due to insufficient insulin release by the pancreas or the inability of body cells to respond effectively to it. This hormone enables the movement of glucose from the bloodstream into cells so that it can be used as energy.

There are two main types of diabetes:

Type 1 Diabetes is an autoimmune disease in which the immune system attacks and destroys beta cells that produce insulin in the pancreas, resulting in little or no insulin production. People with type 1 diabetes must take a lifelong insulin remedy.

Type 2 Diabetes: In this case, the body becomes resistant to insulin or does not produce enough of it. Lifestyle issues like eating habits, exercise and weight gain are very important in managing type 2 diabetes.

Differences Between Type 1 and Type 2 Diabetes

Type 1 Diabetes

Onset and Causes: An autoimmune disorder affects the immune system's functionality. This usually happens during childhood or adolescence, but it can also happen at any age. The immune system goes haywire, leading to the release of antibodies that attack and destroy the beta cells of the pancreas, which are responsible for producing insulin. This results in insufficient insulin levels for the body.

Insulin Dependence: Individuals with Type 1 diabetes are dependent on insulin, meaning they require external administration through injections or a pump to survive.

Symptoms: Often, symptoms come up suddenly, including frequent urination, excessive thirst, increased hunger, unexplained weight loss, fatigue, and blurred vision.

Management: Management of type one diabetes includes regular blood glucose monitoring, taking insulin as prescribed by a doctor, and eating a balanced diet combined with physical activities. Monitoring closely and making changes when necessary will help prevent complications.

Type 2 Diabetes

Onset and Causes: Type 2 diabetes, also known as onset, is more common in adults. However, this disease is increasingly detected among young people because of certain lifestyles, even though it generally occurs in adulthood. This condition arises when the human system cannot use insulin very well or when the pancreas does not make enough insulin to keep blood glucose at normal levels.

Lifestyle Factors: Its risk factors include obesity, physical inactivity, poor diet and genetic predisposition. In contrast with Type 1 diabetes mellitus, however, Type 2 is often preventable through healthy lifestyle choices.

Symptoms: The symptoms are slow to develop and may resemble those of type 1 diabetes. However, they might also include slow-healing sores, frequent infections and darkened areas on the skin, specifically around the neck and armpits.

Management: Management focuses on lifestyle changes such as a healthy diet, regular physical activity and weight loss. Sometimes, medications or insulin injections will be required. Regular blood sugar monitoring ensures that levels remain within target ranges.

The Importance of Diet in Managing Diabetes

Diet plays a crucial role for diabetics. You can have stable glycemia while protecting your overall health status from other complications by making wise dietary decisions whether you have Type 1 or Type 2 diabetes.

Blood sugar control

Carbohydrate Management: Carbohydrates influence blood sugar levels more than any other macronutrient. You must understand which carbohydrates are going into your body before eating them. Complex carbohydrates like vegetables, whole grains, and legumes digest slowly, causing a gradual rise in blood sugars compared to simple sugars and refined carbs.

Glycemic Index: Low GI foods lead to slower increases in blood sugar levels over time. Choosing low-GI foods like non-starchy vegetables, nuts, and certain fruits can help stabilise blood sugar levels.

Weight Management

Calorie Control: For people with Type 2 diabetes, it is important to maintain a healthy weight, as excess body fat, especially around the abdomen, increases insulin resistance. Monitoring calorie intake and choosing healthier foods supports weight loss or maintenance.

Healthy Fats: When your diet includes good fats such as avocados, nuts, seeds and olive oil, you feel satisfied and full, so you are less likely to overeat.

Nutritional Balance

Protein: Lean proteins like chicken, fish, tofu, and legumes help stabilize blood sugar levels while supplying vital nutrients for body repair and maintenance.

Fiber: A high-fiber diet improves glycemic control, lowers cholesterol levels, and aids in weight management. Foods rich in Fiber include whole grains, vegetables, fruits, beans, etc.

Vitamins and Minerals: Maintaining an adequate supply of essential vitamins and minerals promotes general health and helps reduce diabetes-related complications. Magnesium is an example of a mineral found in broccoli nuts and whole wheat bread, and it has been shown to play a role in blood sugar regulation.

Meal Timing and Frequency

Regular Meals help avoid spikes and dips in blood sugar. Blood glucose levels can be kept constant throughout the day by consuming small, balanced meals or snacks every few hours regularly.

Portion Control: Watching portion sizes assists in managing calories and avoiding overfeeding, which is important when controlling weight gain and blood sugar levels.

Individualised Plans

Personalized Diet Plans: Each person suffering from diabetes has unique nutritional requirements. The aim is, therefore, to have meals that have all the necessary elements for effective glucose control in your system while being nutrient-rich; thus, getting guidance from a licensed nutritionist or dietician will help one achieve this goal.

Monitoring and adjustment: Determining how foods affect you individually requires regularly monitoring blood glucose levels. By observing this, people have been able to adjust their diets and improve their diabetes management.

This cookbook is full of different kinds of tasty, low-carb, low-sugar recipes that are just right for those who suffer from diabeteAddingadd these recipes to your meal plan will enable you to eat delicious meals while being able to manage your blood sugar levels efficiently.

Key Nutritional Considerations for Diabetics

Diabetes management requires proper nutrition. Making informed nutritional choices can hugely influence blood sugar control, overall welfare, and quality of life of people with diabetes. Below are a few things about good nutrition for people with diabetes that one should know.

Carbohydrate Management
Types of Carbohydrates: Carbohydrates are a main source of energy, but they affect blood sugar the most. For your diet, it is crucial to know the major distinctions between simple and complex carbohydrates. Simple carbohydrates, such as those in sugary snacks and drinks, cause blood sugar spikes.

Conversely, complex carbohydrates like grains, vegetables and legumes take longer to digest, causing a slight increase in blood sugar levels alone.

Portion Control: It is important to keep track of one's carbohydrate intake. Carbohydrate counting involves calculating how many grams of carbohydrates you eat for every meal to adjust insulin or medication levels needed to control blood sugars. This technique avoids sudden rises in blood sugar, thus maintaining normal glucose concentrations.

Glycaemic Index (GI): Foods are ranked according to their glycaemic index, which shows their impact on blood sugar levels. Low-GI foods, such as non-starchy vegetables, nuts, and some fruits, cause slower, controlled increases in blood sugar. Stabilize your blood sugar by including low-GI foods in your meals.

Protein Intake
Balanced Protein Sources: Protein is essential for repairing and maintaining body tissues, slowing down carbohydrate absorption, and stabilizing blood glucose levels. Lean protein sources like chicken, fish, tofu, and legumes ensure that necessary nutrients are received without excess fat or caloric value.

Plant-Based Proteins: These include beans, lentils, and nuts, which can help improve general health and lower risks associated with diabetes, which usually results in heart disease as a common complication. Such proteins are frequently rich in fiber, which contributes to better control of glucose in the bloodstream.

Healthy Fats
Types of Fats: Not every fat has the same effects when consumed. Some fats support heart health and cut cravings, thus minimizing chances of overeating; an example includes Avocados, among others, which contain monounsaturated fats. This kind of fat can also help to enhance insulin functioning.

Limiting Unhealthy Fats: More cholesterol gets into the blood when saturated fats contained in red meat and full-fat dairy products are eaten, and it is the primary cause of heart disease in most cases. For diabetics, this needs to be limited.

Fiber

High-Fibre Foods: Fiber enhances healthy digestion and maintains normal blood glucose levels. Soluble fiber, present in oats, fruits, vegetables, and legumes, slows glucose absorption, leading to better blood sugar levels. Insoluble fiber, found in whole grains and vegetables, aids in digestion, thereby contributing to satiety.

Daily Fibre Intake: Consume about 25-30 grams of fiber every day. Combining different foods rich in fiber will enhance good glycemic control, which prevents diabetes complications.

Vitamins and minerals

Essential Nutrients: Some vitamins and minerals play specific roles for patients living with diabetes. Magnesium from leafy greens, nuts and whole grains helps with both insulin response and balancing sugar levels in the blood, while chromium obtained from broccoli potatoes, among others, improves an individual's insulin sensitivity.

Antioxidants: Diabetes-related complications, including inflammation, result from oxidative stress; hence, it is vital to eat food rich in antioxidants like berries, nuts or green leaves since they contribute to reducing this condition. Offering your meal variety can help support your health generally.

Hydration

Staying Hydrated: Everyone, including diabetics, needs enough water for proper body functioning. Stable glucose levels are ensured by drinking water without calories added instead of sweetened drinks, which leads to spikes in its content within the bloodstream. Water or herbal teas or any non-caloric beverages

Meal Timing and Frequency

Regular Eating Patterns: Eating at the same time every day can help keep blood glucose levels stable. Consistent meals and snacks can prevent swings in blood sugar and help maintain healthy body weight.

Small, frequent meals: For some individuals, eating smaller but more regular meals is beneficial to stabilize their blood sugars. It also prevents binge eating while managing hunger effectively.

Individualized Plans

Personalized Nutrition: Every individual with diabetes has unique dietary needs. Personalizing your meal plan with a registered dietitian or certified diabetes instructor ensures that your diet accommodates your health goals and lifestyle requirements.

Monitoring and Adjusting: Continuous checks on blood sugar levels help us understand how different foods influence them. Based on such observations, one may be able to adjust one's feeding pattern, leading to better diabetes control and enhanced general health.

The Benefits of Air Frying for Diabetics

Air frying has become increasingly popular as a healthier cooking method, especially for diabetes patients. This technique offers several benefits that align with the dietary and health needs of diabetics. This makes air-frying an excellent choice for people who need better overall health while maintaining normal levels of glucose in their bodies.

Reduced Oil Consumption

One significant advantage of air-frying is that it requires a small quantity of oil or no oil at all. In contrast, traditional frying methods necessitate immersing food in hot oil, which results in a high-fat and calorie-loading meal. Yet air frying uses hot air circulation rather than oil immersion, which means that little or no fat content is added to the food being cooked.

Lower Calorie Intake: Cutting down on oils used during cooking reduces the caloric component in meals, which is pivotal for controlling weight problems among individuals struggling with this condition. Particularly for persons with type 2 diabetes who are prone to insulin resistance due to overweight issues, it is necessary to ensure that the amount of calories consumed does not exceed certain limits.

Healthier Fats: Where oil is required in air-frying, it is often in small quantities. This makes it possible to use healthier oils, such as olive or avocado oil, with good monounsaturated and polyunsaturated fats that promote cardiovascular health and insulin sensitivity.

Better Blood Sugar Control

Air frying results in more stable blood sugar levels than traditional frying methods.

Lower Glycemic Index: Foods cooked with an air fryer generally have a lower glycemic index than their deep-fried counterparts. As a result, these products cause slower blood sugar increases and do not reach dangerous levels for diabetes victims.

Less Carbohydrate Conversion: Deep-frying starchy foods such as potatoes can significantly convert starch into sugar, leading to high glycemic loads. However, these conversions are minimal when using the air-frying technique, making such meals safe for individuals who require stable blood sugars.

Retained Nutrient Content

Air frying helps maintain nutrients. Traditional frying methods, especially those involving high temperatures and long cooking periods, may result in nutrient loss.

Vitamins and Minerals: Air frying retains essential vitamins and nutrients better than the traditional method. Even after being cooked, some nutrients like vitamin C, potassium, and antioxidants remain, thus maintaining a healthy diet for people with diabetes.

Fibre Preservation: The hot air method helps maintain the Fibre content in vegetables and other foodstuffs. Fiber plays a key role among diabetics since it slows down the process of sugars entering the bloodstream, promoting improved blood glucose control systems.

Enhanced Flavour and Texture

Air frying produces foods that are crispy on the outside and juicy on the inside, like deep-fried food, but without using too much oil and adding calories.

Appealing Meals: Finding interesting and satisfying meals is important for people with diabetes. Air frying enables one to have that delicious taste in crisply made food while ensuring that one remains healthy, avoiding the wrong diet for persons suffering from diabetes.

Versatility: The air fryer is multipurpose, as it can be used to make different kinds of food, such as fruits, vegetables, snacks and even desserts.

This variation helps to avoid boredom in eating and maintain long-term adherence to an appropriate diet.

Convenience and Safety

Air fryers are handy kitchen tools that come with several user-friendly features regarding their security levels.

Ease of Use: They are simple to use, and some have pre-set cooking times and temperatures, thus making it easy for someone who wants to cook fast so as not to waste time. This can be essential, particularly for busy individuals who lack confidence in cooking techniques.

Safety: Air frying minimizes accidents related to hot oil, such as burns, fires, etc. It is especially important for people with diabetes who may also develop neuropathy (damage to blood vessels).

Reduced Formation of Harmful Compounds

Traditional frying processes can lead to the formation of toxic substances such as acrylamide, a potential carcinogen formed during high-temperature cooking of starchy foods.

Lower Acrylamide Levels: Generally, air-frying reduces acrylamide content compared with deep frying. This reduction in harmful compounds is an added health benefit, particularly for individuals with diabetes who are at an increased risk of developing other health issues.

Environmental and Economic Benefits

Additionally, there are environmental benefits associated with air fryers alongside economic ones.

Energy Efficiency: They usually use less energy than ordinary ovens or deep fryers. They preheat rapidly and cook faster, thus making them more energy efficient.

Cost Savings: Air frying can save money over time using less oil and energy. In addition, because air fryers are durable and have multi-use capacity, they can replace other kitchen appliances.

Supporting a Balanced Diet

Air-frying supports a balanced diet as it allows for the preparation of low-fat versions of traditionally fried foods, allowing you to enjoy different foods without compromising on your nutritional goals.

Healthy Alternatives: Most significantly, an air fryer helps create more nutritious options like vegetables made in an air fryer instead of the traditional fried ones, lean proteins, and even baked air-fried desserts. This facilitates easier adherence to a well-balanced diet that is good for patients with diabetes while providing tasty meals.

Getting Started with Your Air Fryer

Why Choose an Air Fryer?

Beyond the health benefits mentioned before, when choosing kitchen appliances, air fryers are special. Here are some reasons why you might choose an air fryer for your cooking:

Versatility

Air fryers are one of the most diverse cooking equipment and can perform several cooking tasks. From roasting and grilling to baking anything you think of, the air fryer does multi-purposing. This offers you a chance to prepare different meals without so many kitchen appliances. This appliance includes crispy vegetables, tender meats, baked goods, and snacks.

Quick & Effective Cooking

Meals cooked in air fryers cook fast and efficiently. They use fast-moving hot air that cooks food uniformly, so their cooking time is usually shorter than that of traditional ovens. Therefore, if you're always in a hurry, preparing meals in an air fryer will be convenient for you. Additionally, they take very little prep time, meaning that nearly shortly after turning it on, you start cooking.

Ease of Use

The functionality of frying machines has been made easy for anyone to use. First-time cooks can still get flawless results because most models have simple controls and factory settings for basic dishes. The digital screens and touchpads on many frying devices make them more user-friendly by enabling users to set accurate heat levels and timings with only minimal taps.

Compact Design

These kinds of appliances are small, so they should not be avoided by households with limited spaces, particularly smaller kitchens. However, despite occupying small areas, they can hold surprisingly large amounts of food, meaning they can be used both during small meal times or large family dinners. Further, since they're portable, one could easily store them away whenever not required, even carrying them along while out camping.

Energy Efficiency

These machines consume less energy compared to normal ovens. This means that the heating up is faster, and the temperature remains constant, leading to energy savings over a long duration. This feature can save on electricity bills and also make them environmentally friendly; hence, they are good for your kitchen.

Easy Cleanup

Ease of cleaning is one of the most appreciated features of an air fryer. Most air fryers come with non-stick pans and accessories that allow you to save time since they are dishwashable.

This means you will never be required to clean off everything after a meal when you want homemade food.

Consistent Results
They give out uniform cooking results, which is why these machines are called air fryers. The heat from above circulates evenly through the entire cooking chamber, which implies that there is no chance of leaving some parts uncooked or overcooking them. This aspect helps ensure the right structure and taste at all times, improving your confidence in the kitchen and culinary skills.

Safety Features
Today's versions come with safety features like automatic switch-off, cool-touch handles, or anti-slip feet, among others, to prevent accidents in case anything goes wrong. The presence of children or elderly adults in families makes it much easier if a family uses an air fryer because it reduces the risk.

Cost-Effective
Although the cost of an air fryer can differ at first, it is one of the most cost-effective devices because of its versatility and the money saved from the reduced use of oil and electricity. Furthermore, using an air fryer to cook at home saves more money than regular takeout or dining out.

Healthier Cooking Methods
As previously said, the idea that this appliance can make healthier food without sacrificing taste is important for everyone considering buying it. That way, it helps maintain a healthy lifestyle and fits into certain diets, especially those individuals with diabetes and other ailments.

Encourages Home Cooking
An Air Fryer could encourage more cooking at home because it's convenient, fast, and versatile. This allows for meals to be better controlled with respect to ingredients used, portion sizes and nutritional contents, which are all important in assisting people with diabetes to manage blood glucose levels, among other things. By making cooking fun and accessible, air fryers stimulate healthier eating habits, leading to a healthier life.

Innovative Technology
Air fryers are equipped with state-of-the-art technology that continues to evolve. The latest iterations might feature functions such as smart links enabling you to run them through your phone. In contrast, others have multiple-use potentials where they are integrated into pressure cookers or toaster ovens among others. This kind of innovation ensures that you acquire a top-notch tool that will meet modern cooking demands.

Choosing an Air Fryer offers several practical, economical and culinary benefits for your kitchen area. Its versatility, efficiency, ease of use and health benefits make it a valuable addition for anyone seeking to improve their cooking skills while maintaining good nutrition. Whether you're experienced in the kitchen or not, owning an air fryer could help you make tasty, healthy foods effortlessly.

Air Fryer Basics: How It Works

Because they offer healthier cooking methods compared to traditional frying techniques, there is no doubt that air fryers have revolutionized home cooking. Understanding the functioning of air fryers will help you optimize their usefulness in your kitchen. Below is an in-depth look at what defines an air fryer, how it functions, and what makes it tick.

The Core Technology: Rapid Air Circulation

Rapid air circulation technology is at the heart of all air fryers, and this is how they work. This technique imitates profound frying effects by blowing hot air around the food at high velocity. The procedure can be broken down as below:

Heating Element: In most cases, a powerful heating element is located on top of the appliance. This element heats the air inside its cooking chamber very fast to any temperature between 180°F and 400°F (82°C and 204°C).

Fan: A high-speed fan directly above or around the heating element forces hot air down to the food during cooking. The circulation of heated air ensures that every side of the food gets cooked perfectly with a crisp exterior yet tender inside.

Cooking Chamber: The cooking chamber in an Air Fryer has been designed to facilitate the free flow of hot air. It commonly contains perforated baskets or trays for even airflow distribution over grilled food. Therefore, just like a convection oven but faster- from all directions, foods will be cooked using such a design of the chamber itself.

Exhaust System: Air fryers have exhaust systems to manage the pressure and temperature in the appliance. The exhaust releases too much hot air and filters out any steam or smoke, keeping the appliance clean and safe for cooking.

Key Components of an Air Fryer

Understanding the main components of an air fryer will help you in effectively using and maintaining your device as follows;

Control Panel: Most air fryers have a control panel that allows you to set the desired temperature and timing depending on your cooking. This may be digital or analogue, depending on the model. Some advanced models come with pre-set cooking programs for common foods like fries, chicken, and vegetables, which make it easier to achieve perfect results with less effort.

Basket or Tray: These are where food is placed. They can usually be removed, and holes are all over them for maximum airflow. Some models come with several trays or racks so that one can cook various foods at the same time without getting mixed up.

Pan: The tray catches any drippings or fat that drop during cooking, keeping them from falling onto the basket or tray below. This helps prevent oil residues from catching fire, hence keeping off smoky smells from burnt fats.

Handle: This is designed so users can insert the basket without getting burned by hot oil. It's meant to remain cool despite having hot contents.

Outer Body: With its outer body covering all parts, unlike other designs, it normally remains cool throughout use. This aspect helps avoid burns, making it suitable for every kitchen countertop.

Operating an Air Fryer: Step-by-Step Guide

Using an air fryer is straightforward; this includes:

Preheating: Some recipes require air fryers to be preheated before starting cooking in order to obtain the best results. Set up your temperature control and let your air fryer run for a couple of minutes before adding your foodstuff. Then, allow your oven to reach its desired temperature for cooking evenly.

Prepare Your Food: While the air fryer is preheating, prepare your food. Cut ingredients into uniform sizes to ensure even cooking. If desired, lightly brush some oil onto the food. This step can enhance the crispiness of the final product without adding excessive calories.

Loading the Basket: You can now put the prepared food in this basket or tray. Ensure each piece has enough space so hot air can move freely around it. For larger quantities, cook them separately and not all together to get better results at all times.

Set Time and Temperature: Use the control panel to set the right temperature and cooking time based on your recipe. For common food items, most air fryers come with pre-set programs, while others allow you to adjust them manually as needed.

Cooking: Start the air fryer after you have set it up. It will circulate hot air around the food as it cooks to perfection. For even browning, shake or flip halfway through cooking.

Checking for Doneness: As you near the completion of your cooking time, check for doneness. Most of these devices have a pause button that allows you to open the basket and check on the food without resetting your timer. If it is not quite done, close the basket and let it continue cooking.

Maintenance and Cleaning

Properly maintaining and cleaning your air fryer is important if you want it to remain in good working condition.

Cool Down: Before beginning any maintenance process with regards to this device, give it enough time until its entire surface has cooled off. This way no burning and protects nonstick coating of basket and pan.

Disassemble: Remove the basket, tray, and pan from the air fryer. These parts may be dishwasher-friendly however always confirm using manufacturers' instructions first.

Clean the Basket and Tray: Rinse them using warm soapy water; Using non-abrasive sponges will prevent spoiling their non-stick coat; And have some minutes or soaks at particular sections just in case they persistently stick or resist wiping off.

Wipe the Interior and Exterior: A wet cloth should be used when sanitizing both interior plus exterior parts of this frying device since utilizing abrasive materials or rough chemicals could ruin them instead.

Reassemble: Assemble the appliance again once all the parts are clean and dry. You must ensure that everything is in place before storing or using it again.

Essential Tips for Air Frying

Air frying can change how you cook by providing a healthier option to enjoying your best dishes. To maximize your use of air fryer, consider these essential tips:

1. Preheat Your Air Fryer
Consistent Results: It is important to preheat this appliance to the desired temperature prior to cooking so as to achieve evenness in the texture and thorough cooking.

Time-Saver: In addition, preheating will save you some overall time spent on cooking since food gets prepared much faster.

2. Don't Overcrowd the Basket
Air Circulation: Overcrowding the basket can restrict air flow making it impossible for even cooking. There should be enough space between each food item to allow hot air pass through freely around them.

Batch Cooking: You may also choose to prepare food in several batches only if there is too much of it. This guarantees uniformity in cooking tendency that yields a crispy outcome desired thus far.

3. Shake or Flip Food Halfway

Even Cooking: Shaking or flipping the food halfway through the cooking process promotes even browning and crisping, which is especially crucial when preparing fries, chicken wings, vegetables etc.

Check Doneness: Another purpose of shaking midway is assessing if what you are doing has already made sense at all or not.

4. Use a Light Coating of Oil
Enhance Crispiness: One cannot use too much oil but lightly brushing food with oil will make them crispy when cooked in an air fryer. You can use cooking spray or brush on some oil.

Healthier Options: Choose olive, avocado or coconut oils that are good for your health and taste nice as well.

5. Adjust Cooking Times and Temperatures
Recipe Variations: The size, type, and brand along with the model of your air fryer determines its cooking times and temperatures.
Start at a Lower Temperature First: Lower temperatures are preferred because they guard against scorching food while giving you more control over the cooking process.

6. Use Air Fryer-Safe Accessories

Expand Cooking Options: With things like baking pans, grilling racks, skewers etc., you can go beyond what your air fryer is made to do. It would be best if you only used those which are marked "air fryer safe" so as not to spoil your appliance.

They Will Improve Your Food: Such add-ons will help you in getting various recipes better like kebabs, multi layers dishes or cakes for example.

7. Season Food Before Cooking

Making Taste Better: To let flavors seep into food while being processed put different seasonings before frying in an air fryer; spice up with herbs as you desire.

Avoid Wet Battering: A moist batter may not work well in an air-fryer therefore dry coats or very light crumbs give the crispiest texture possible instead of wet ones.

8. Clean Your Air Fryer Regularly

Maintain Performance: Keeping this appliance clean will ensure it works efficiently and holds out longer. After each time you cook anything using it don't forget about wiping out a basket, tray and pan from leftovers of meals thereon and fats.

Do Not Use Harsh Chemicals: Use mild non-abrasive detergents and a soft sponge. Remember that most of the constituents can be cleaned using a dishwasher, but it is better to refer to the manufacturer's guidelines.

9. Monitor Cooking Progress

You Should Check on It Often: Different foods have different cooking times so sometimes when you are frying you need to check them. In case they overcook, taste and their texture may become unsatisfactory for eating purposes.

Adjust as Needed: You don't need to stick with the original time or temperature, just make sure your dish is ready even if it requires minor adjustments. The final result in a kitchen depends on marginal corrections.

10. Experiment with Recipes

Try New Foods: With an air fryer at home you'll always have an opportunity to try out new ingredients and some recipes too; fries only should not be limiting you, go beyond that by trying roasted veggies, baked foodstuff as well as making desserts occasionally.

11. Use Aluminium Foil or Parchment Paper Wisely

Prevent Sticking: Lining the basket with aluminium foil or parchment paper is the best way to keep food from sticking while frying as well as maintaining its cleanliness after use. However there should be no obstruction of flow of air.

Avoid Blocking Air Flow: Ensure there is free movement of air in the basket hence do not cover all sides using liners – create holes or buy perforated parchment papers designed for air fryers instead.

12. Allow Food to Rest
Redistribute Juices: Resting cooked mealtime allows juices distribute into the meat resulting in tastier and juicier meals like steaks or pork chops.
Cool Down: This provides the food with an opportunity to cool slightly and make it safer and more appetizing.

13. Keep the Air Fryer in a Ventilated Area
Heat Dissipation: Put your air fryer on a heat resistant surface that is flat and ventilated. Avoid placing it close to walls or other devices which could impede its flow of air.

Prevent Overheating: The right ventilation will prevent the unit from overheating during operations thereby ensuring safety.

14. Follow the Manufacturer's Instructions
Optimal Use: Specific instructions and recommendations may apply differently to different models of air fryers. Be sure to refer to this booklet for guidance on how to use your air fryer properly.
Warranty Protection: In addition, following instructions can protect your warranty while making sure that you obtain optimal performance from this important kitchen appliance.

Cleaning and Maintenance of Your Air Fryer

Keeping your air fryer in good condition guarantees its efficiency as well as durability. You preserve health by maintaining cleanliness of home appliances and also keep your meals in good quality. This article provides you with complete instruction on how to clean and maintain your great kitchen appliance, which is known as an air fryer:

1. Unplug and Cool Down
Safety First: Prior initiating any cleaning activity, always unplug for cooling purposes till fully cooled down. These help avoid electrical injuries and burns.
Cool Down: In case you decide to engage in cleaning activities after some time, ensure that all components have cooled down before starting to clean them or anything else that might get affected afterwards.

2. Disassemble the Components
Take Out Parts Such As Basket And Tray: Remove parts such as the basket, tray, and pan from within the cooking chamber since they're typically removable making cleaning much easier.
Handle With Care: Delicately remove these parts so that you don't scratch off their non-stick coating or destroy other delicate parts.

3. Clean the Basket and Tray
Hand Wash: The basket and tray can be cleaned using warm soapy water and a non-abrasive sponge. Avoid use of harsh chemicals or steel wool as these will damage the non-stick coating.
Soak Stubborn Residues: On stubborn residues, let the basket and tray soak in warm soapy water for about 10 to 15 minutes before scrubbing them. By doing this, all solid particles that are stuck on it can become loose.

Dishwasher Safe: Most air fryer baskets and trays can be washed using a dishwasher. Check the manufacturer's instructions if you are not sure, then place them inside the machine for a thorough washing.

4. Clean the Pan
Wipe And Rinse: After every use, clean the pan which collects drippings and excess oil by wiping it with paper towel to remove oil before washing with warm soapy water.
Avoid Scratches: Use soft sponges while cleaning to avoid scratches on its surface. Alternatively, if it is dishwasher safe, just do so.

5. Wipe Down the Interior
Remove Debris: Check whether there is any food debris or grease splatters inside your air fryer while wiping its interior surfaces using moist damp clothes or sponges.

Mild Detergent: Mix mild detergent with water especially where spots are difficult to clean up. Do not apply any abrasive cleaners or scouring pads to prevent any damages from occurring within its insides.

Dry Thoroughly: Assemble only after making sure that its internal components have completely dried out in order to prevent moulds or mildew from growing in such places again.

6. Clean the Heating Element
Delicate Cleaning: On top of the cooking compartment, there is a heating element that accumulates grease and food particles as time goes by. Use a soft brush or cloth to clean it gently.

Avoid Water: Never pour water directly on the heating element but use a moistened cloth instead wiping it gently.

7. Exterior Cleaning
Wipe Down: Get a damp cloth and wipe the exterior part of your air fryer. Pay attention to touch areas like handle and control panel.

Mild Soap: When necessary, you can use mild soap solution to eliminate any fat or spots. You should be sure not to let water reach any electrical parts such as control panel section.

8. Reassemble and Store
Dry Components: Before you put back together your air fryer ensure all components are completely dry otherwise moisture will result in mold growth or even damage your appliance.

Proper Storage: Keep your air fryer in a dry cool area making sure it's well cleaned and dried off completely so that no odors or molds start developing.

9. Regular Maintenance Tips
Check for Wear and Tear: The basket, tray, pan should be regularly observed for signs of wearing out by peeling or chipping off non-stick coating which may suggest that it's time to replace them.

Ventilation: For protection against overheating make sure that your air fryer has enough ventilation during cooking process; the vents should also be kept open whilst regular cleaning is necessary for proper airflow through them.

Odor Removal: If your air fryer starts having a smell coming from inside of it then running some water/lemon juice mixtures through it for about five minutes would help get rid of such smells forever.

Descale if Needed: In case you reside in an area where there is hard water descaling could help in maintaining its efficiency once in a while. Remove mineral deposits with vinegar solution wash up.

10. Deep Cleaning Tips
Quarterly Cleaning: After every few months, it is important to do a deep clean of the air fryer, especially if you use it frequently. This involves thorough cleaning of all parts and making sure no grease or food particles are left behind.

Use a Brush: Use a soft brush for areas that cannot be reached with ease when you want to get rid of dirt. It is particularly effective in clearing the fan and the heating element.

Cleaning Solutions: If necessary, you can always find specialized cleaners meant for kitchen appliances. Follow instructions from manufacturer on safe use for efficient cleanliness.

11. Troubleshooting Common Issues
Uneven Cooking: Ensure that the basket is not overfilled and that your air fryer is neat if you discover that your meal does not cook well. Also, this could result from blockage of an air vent or a damaged fan.

Smoke or Odor: Your air fryer might be producing smoke or having strong smell because there is too much oil or food remnants getting burnt inside it; ensure that it's thoroughly cleaned and also do not apply excess fats while cooking.

Electrical Issues: In case the fryer fails to switch on/off for electrical reasons like power cord issues first examine any loose connection problems by inspecting plug as well as socket status plus ensure proper working outlet selection by plugging into it rather than others not functioning correctly. If trouble still persists approach company involved for help.

Low-Carb, Low-Sugar Cooking: The Fundamentals

Cooking low-carb and low-sugar meals is important in managing diabetes effectively. Knowing the basics of this style of cooking will help you make delicious and nutritious dishes that work for your health goals. Here's a comprehensive guide to the basics of low-carb, low-sugar cooking:

Understanding Carbohydrates and Sugars

Types of Carbohydrates

Simple Carbohydrates: Simple carbohydrates which can be found in foods like fruits, honey, and dairy products are broken down easily by the body thus they cause rapid increases in blood sugar.

Complex Carbohydrates: These are contained in whole grains, legumes as well as vegetables. This takes longer to digest; hence, blood sugars stabilize over time.

Sugars

Natural Sugars: Natural sugars are fruits found in fruits and dairy products. Although these natural sugars have an effect on blood sugar levels, they contain nutrients such as Fiber vitamins.

Added Sugars: These include those added to food during processing or preparation including those present in sugary drinks, desserts and most processed foods. Thus it is vital to minimize intake of added sugars if one has diabetes.

Key Principles of Low-Carb, Low-Sugar Cooking

1. Choose Whole, Unprocessed Foods
Nutrient Density: Whole foods including vegetables lean proteins nuts seeds tend to be nutrient dense, lower in carbohydrates/sugars than processed foods.

Avoid Additives: processed foods may have hidden sugars or unhealthy fats; therefore making a choice for whole foods helps you avoid them hence better control over carbs/sugars intake.

2. Focus on Fiber
Blood Sugar Control: Fibre slows down the breakdown and absorption rate of carbohydrates leading to more stable blood sugar levels so try adding high-Fibre foods like vegetables legumes & whole grains into your plate when eating meals.

Satiety: Apart from being satisfying high-Fibre diets make people feel full longer reducing the urge to snack on high-carb or sugary foods.

3. Incorporate Healthy Fats
Satisfaction: Flavor and satisfaction are added to your meals by healthy fats such as avocados nuts seeds olive oil without raising blood sugar levels.

Nutrient Absorption: Fats help with the absorption of fat-soluble vitamins (A, D, E, & K) from our foods thereby enhancing overall nutrition.

4. Lean Proteins are Key
Muscle Maintenance: proteins are important for muscle maintenance and general body health; thus choosing lean sources like chicken/turkey/fish/tofu/legumes is recommended.

Satiety due to Presence of Protein in Meal and Blood Sugar Level Stabilization: Your chances of getting spikes become minimal if there is protein in your meal that will keep you full and maintain a constant glucose level .

5. Use Natural Sweeteners Sparingly
Alternative Sweeteners: To substitute sugar naturally stevia erythritol monk fruit etc. which can be used sparingly so as to satisfy one's craving naturally while not affecting sugar levels negatively.

Limit Use: However, they must be limited due to low carbohydrate content for one who wants a balanced diet.

Practical Tips for Low-Carb, Low-Sugar Cooking

1. Plan Your Meals
Weekly Planning: This way you can ensure that your diet continues to remain low in carbs/sugars plus makes better food choices throughout the week.

Grocery List: Make a shopping list based on your meal plan this avoids impulse buys of high-carbohydrate or high-sugar items at the store..

2. Cooking Techniques
Grilling And Baking: These methods allow proteins and vegetables to be cooked without adding extra carbohydrates or sugars.

Steaming And Sautéing : Steaming helps retain nutrients in vegetables while sautéed with healthy fats adds taste without extra carbohydrates.

3. Spice It Up

Herbs and spices: Utilize a combination of spices and herbs in your meals to add taste without salt or sugar. Some of the options include garlic, ginger, turmeric, and rosemary.

Home-made Seasonings: Create your own spice blends to avoid unhealthy additives and additional sweeteners present in purchased varieties.

4. Smart Swaps
Vegetable Noodles: To bring down the level of carbohydrates you consume, try substituting zucchini noodles or spaghetti squash instead of regular pasta.

Cauliflower Rice: Use cauliflower rice instead of normal rice for lower carb intake.

Leafy Greens: Replace tortillas or bread with large leafy greens such as lettuce or collards as wrap-ups.

5. Be Mindful of Sauces and Dressings
Homemade Versions: Most store-bought sauces and dressings have hidden sugars within them. By making your version allows you to choose what goes into it.

Low-Sugar Options: For commercial varieties, go for those marked low-sugar or sugar-free while always checking the back label.

Creating Balanced Meals

1. Plate Method
Half Veggies: Fill half your dinner plate with non-starchy vegetables such as leafy greens, broccoli, peppers, and cucumbers.

Quarter Protein: A quarter of your plate should be reserved for lean protein.

Quarter Whole Grains: When selecting grains, choose whole grain and let them take one-quarter of the plate so that you can control the carbohydrate content.

2. Portion Control
Smaller Plates: When serving yourself food on small plates you will help control portion sizes and prevent overeating.

Mindful Eating: Being mindful about eating is important because it helps in recognizing signs of fullness or hunger always. By eating slowly while enjoying every bite, one is able to avoid taking more than enough carbs and sugars.

3. Balanced Snacks

Protein and Fiber: Go for snacks containing both proteins and fibers like a handful of nuts; some fruit combined with nut butter or veggie sticks together with hummus.

Avoid Sugary Snacks: Avoid sweetened snacks such as candy, bakery products or sugary drinks.

4. Hydration
Water First: Choose water as your main drink because it helps to quench thirst without adding more calories into your body. By staying hydrated you are also able to minimize hunger pangs thereby reducing the chances of consuming high carb or even sugary drinks.

Infused Water: If plain water does not excite you, try cucumber, lemon slices or berries infused water for a refreshing taste.

How to Modify Recipes for Diabetic Needs

Adapting recipes to suit diabetic dietary needs may appear complex but with a few modifications; it is possible to enjoy various tasty dishes in line with one's health objectives. Here are some tips on how to change recipes so they are suitable for people with diabetes:

Understanding the Basics

1. Focus on the Glycemic Index (GI)
Low-GI Foods: Look out for ingredients that are low in glycemic index (GI) and are absorbed slowly to help maintain stable blood sugar levels. Examples include whole grains, legumes, and non-starchy vegetables.

Avoid High-GI Foods: The ones that have high GI such as white bread, white rice and sweet snacks should be rarely consumed since they cause a rapid rise in the level of glucose in the blood.

2. Balance Macronutrients
Carbohydrates: Keep an eye on carbohydrate content by substituting high carb foods for low-carb alternatives in your recipes.

Proteins: To control blood sugar levels while also feeling full, choose proteins from lean sources like eggs or fish.

Fats: Enhance taste and nutrition by incorporating healthy fats sourced from avocados, nuts or olive oil into cooking.

Substituting Ingredients

1. Replace Refined Carbs
Whole Grains: Choose whole grain versions like quinoa, brown rice or whole wheat pasta instead of refined grains such as white rice and pasta.

Vegetable Alternatives: When making spaghetti strands or rice there can be vegetable substitutes such as zucchini noodles, cauliflower rice or spaghetti squash among others.

2. Reduce Sugar
Natural Sweeteners: Instead of using sugar use other natural sweeteners such as stevia, monk fruit or erythritol which do not increase blood sugar levels significantly.

Fruit Purees: Fruits like apple sauce or mashed bananas can give natural sweetness and moisture to pastry when pureed before addition to dough.

3. Choose Healthy Fats
Cooking Oils: Change unhealthy fats like butter with healthier oils such as olive oil, avocado oil or coconut oil for cooking purposes only.

Dairy Alternatives: Unsweetened almond milk, coconut milk and Greek yoghurt may replace high fat dairy products when used in baking cakes.

4. Increase Fibre Content
Flaxseeds and Chia Seeds: Add ground flaxseeds or chia seeds to recipes to boost dietary fiber content and better control blood sugar.

Vegetables: Include more non-starchy vegetables in your meals to include Fibre and nutrients without increasing carbs drastically.

Cooking Techniques

1. Baking and Grilling
Healthy ways: Bake, grill, steam or roast rather than fry to use less oil and keep the food benefits intact.

Seasoning: Get flavor from herbs, spices as well as citrus juices instead of sugar or unhealthy fats.

2. Portion Control
Decrease Portions: Offering small quantities of the meal will assist in ensuring that carbohydrate intake is managed well while eliminating spikes of blood-glucose levels.

Measuring Tools: Use measuring cups and spoons for precise measurement of ingredients as well as portion control.

Adapting Specific Recipes

1. Breakfast Dishes
Pancakes and Waffles: Use almond flour or coconut flour instead of regular flour. Also, add mashed bananas or pureed pumpkin for natural sweetness.

Oatmeal: Instead of instant oats, go for steel-cut oats or rolled oats. Replace sugar with fresh berries, nuts and a sprinkle of cinnamon on top.

2. Main Courses
Stir-Fries: Utilize cauliflower rice or a mix of vegetables instead of white rice. For example, you can use lean proteins like chicken, tofu or shrimp along with low sodium soy sauce.

Pasta Dishes: Instead of pasta, take out spiralized zucchini or spaghetti squash from your pantry. Additionally, make sauces using fresh tomatoes & herbs plus a touch olive oil instead of creamy and sugary varieties.

3. Desserts
Baked Goods: Alternatively replace wheat flour with almond flour/coconut flour; sweeten desserts with monk fruit/stevia without artificial sweeteners; incorporate nuts/seeds/dark chocolate (70% cocoa content) for extra taste/texture.

Fruit-Based Desserts: Focus on fruit-based desserts such as baked apples or berry parfaits with Greek yogurt; lightly dress them up wih a splash of lemon juice and mint.

4. Snacks
Healthy Alternatives: Choose snacks that combine protein and fiber, like hummus with veggie sticks, Greek yogurt with a handful of nuts, or an apple with peanut butter.

Homemade Options: Instead of buying snacks from the store which are often filled with added sugars and unhealthy fats make your own batch of homemade trail mix that contains nuts, seeds and just a little dried fruit.

Monitoring and Adjusting

1. Blood Sugar Testing
Frequent Monitoring: Regularly test your blood sugar levels especially after preparing new meals. This way you will have the chance to understand how various foods affect your blood glucose levels.

Adjustments: Make necessary changes based on your blood glucose reading. For instance, if the recipe causes a spike in blood sugar try reducing portion size or modifying one or two ingredients.

2. Consult a Dietitian
Professional Guidance: Find a registered dietitian who can help you modify recipes and develop meal plans tailored to your specific needs.

Personalized Advice: A dietitian can provide personalized advice on ingredient substitutions, portion sizes, and meal timing to help you better manage your diabetes.

Practical Examples

1. Classic Lasagna
Noodle Replacement: Use thinly sliced zucchini or eggplant instead of traditional lasagna noodles.

Sauce and Cheese: Making marinara sauce with low-carbs using fresh tomatoes Herbs; use mozzarella cheese plus part-skim ricotta to decrease fat content.

2. Homemade Pizza
Crust Alternative: Choose cauliflower crusts or whole wheat tortillas as alternatives for making pizza doughs.

Toppings: Load up on non-starchy veggies; use lean proteins such as grilled chicken or turkey while still including some cheese.

3. Sweet Treats
Chocolate Chip Cookies: Replace flour with almond flour/sugar with natural sweetener such as stevia/ add dark chocolate chips for fewer sugar cookies.

Smoothies: Blend with unsweetened almond milk, a handful of spinach, some berries and a scoop of protein powder. Do not add fruit juices or sweetened yogurt.

Portion Control and Meal Planning

Effective diabetes management entails more than just right dieting; it demands careful portion control and structured meal planning. These practices help in maintaining steady blood sugar levels, preventing spikes, and promoting overall health. Here is how to approach portion control and meal planning for a diabetic-friendly diet:

Portion Control

1. Understanding Serving Sizes
Reading Labels: Read food labels to learn about standard serving sizes. Be sure to take note of the portions indicated on food packages and adjust your intake accordingly.

Visual Cues: To estimate portions, use visual cues while preparing meals. For example, A serving size of meat should be about the size of a deck of cards whereas one serving of pasta should have an approximate size equal to that of a baseball.

2. Using Measuring Tools
Measuring Cups and Spoons: Use measuring cups or spoons when working in the kitchen with high-carb foods to measure ingredients accurately.

Food Scale: Invest in a food scale if you are concerned about portion sizes mainly for items like meats, cheeses or anything dense.

3. Plate Method
Balanced Plate: Design balanced meals using the plate method where half your plate consists non-starchy vegetables, one quarter has lean protein while the other holds whole grains/starchy vegetables.

Smaller Plates: Use small plates to help manage portion sizes – this can make your mind think you are satisfied after eating less food.

4. Mindful Eating
Slow Down: Eat slowly and savor each bite; this will give you time to realize when you're full before overeating occurs.bbbb Avoid Distractions such as TV or phones during meals so that you can concentrate on your body's hunger signals as well as the food itself.

Meal Planning

1. Plan Ahead
Weekly Planning: Plan a weekly meal schedule that includes breakfast, lunch, dinner, and snacks. It can help to ensure that your diet is balanced and prevent you from making unhealthy choices.

Grocery List: To stay organized and avoid spontaneous purchases based on your cravings or appetite, make a grocery list according to the planned meals.

2. Balanced Meals
Macronutrient Balance: Make sure each meal has carbohydrates proteins fat in it so as to maintain the balance of stable blood sugar level while providing long-lasting energy.

Fiber-Rich Foods: Incorporate vegetables, legumes and whole grains in your diet to increase fibre intake which is good for digestion and will lower your blood sugar levels.

3. Portion Sizes
Pre-Portion Snacks: Prepare and portion out snacks ahead of time to avoid overeating. Small containers or snack bags are great for nuts, fruits, vegetables etc.

Batch Cooking: Cook large quantities of food in one go rather than separate portions so that it can be easily picked up throughout the week without much fuss.

4. Monitor Carbohydrate Intake
Carb Counting: Keep a record of how many carbs are in each meal; this specifically important for people who use insulin because they need to adjust their dosage accordingly.

Low-Carb Substitutes: For ingredients high in carbohydrates such as rice or pasta try using low-carb alternatives like cauliflower rice or zucchini noodles instead.

5. Timing and Frequency
Regular Intervals: Eat at regular intervals instead of waiting until you're starving so that your body doesn't go into starvation mode where binging becomes difficult to avoid sometimes overeating happens if we skipped a meal thus should not be done away with completely .

Consistent Timing: Establish routine by eating at the same time every day –this might also help regulate insulin production as well as glucose levels therefore maintaining steady blood sugar levels all through.

Adjusting Meal Plans
1. Flexibility
Substitute Ingredients: Feel free to substitute ingredients as long as the macronutrient balance is maintained and considering availability and personal preference.

Variety: Use variety to ensure that you don't only include a range of nutrients but also avoid monotony in your meals.

2. Adjust for Activity Levels

Active Days: On more active days, consider having slightly larger portions or an extra snack in order to keep up with energy requirements?

Less Active Days: On less active days, be aware of portion sizes and choose lighter meals and snacks?

Special Occasions
Plan Ahead: For special occasions or dining out, plan by having smaller balanced meals earlier in the day and checking the menu beforehand for healthier options.

Stocking Your Pantry with Diabetic-Friendly Ingredients

When trying to maintain a healthy diet it is important that you have a well stocked pantry filled with diabetic-friendly ingredients. Having these ingredients on hand can make it easier for you to cook healthy low-carb, low-sugar meals without any major hassle. Here's how you can stock your pantry with foods that suit your dietary needs:

Whole Grains and Legumes

1. Whole Grains

Quinoa: It is high fiber grain-like foodstuff rich in protein.
Brown Rice: It has a higher nutritional value compared with white rice because it is considered as whole grain.
Whole Wheat Pasta An alternative version of refined pasta offering more Fibre and other nutrients.
Steel-Cut Oats: Lower glycemic index than rolled or instant oats because they are less processed.
Barley: This grain has high Fiber content making it perfect for soups and salads.

2. Legumes

Chickpeas: Roasted, made into hummus or salads – they are so versatile!
Lentils: These are excellent choices for stews or soups since they contain both proteins and fibers.
Black Beans: Also, salads and soups can be enriched with these.
Kidney Beans: They work well in chili and other hearty dishes.
Nuts, Seeds, and Healthy Fats

1. Nuts
Almonds: They contain proteins and healthy fats; you can eat them raw on their own or add to your recipe when cooking.

Walnuts: These have a lot of omega-3 fatty acids which are very good for your health in general terms.

Pistachios: You can eat them alone or add to any dish as they have high protein content and dietary fiber?

2. Seeds

Chia Seeds: Fibre content in Chia Seeds is high, omega 3s too making them perfect for use in smoothies; yogurt etc

Flaxseeds: Added to smoothies cereal extra Fibre ground flaxseeds could be used for baking cakes, muffins etc.

Pumpkin Seeds: This is also a great snack or topping option when you prepare oatmeal or salads at home.

3. Healthy Fats

Olive Oil: For both cooking and salad dressings besides marinating.

Avocado Oil: When preparing salads or cooking things over high heat this oil can be very useful?

Coconut Oil: It has specific fragrance but still it must be used moderately when we bake something or fry food with it!

4. Proteins

1. Canned Fish

Tuna fish packed in water would be best so as to reduce fat addition through canned varieties that could have been preserved otherwise.

Salmon is rich in heart healthy omega 3 fatty acids.

Sardines are another excellent source of omega-3 fatty acids that may also act as calcium supplements while adding flavor if added into salads just like tuna tin ones found at local supermarket.

2. Plant-Based Proteins

Tofu: A type of protein that has a wide range of uses such as soups stir fries and salads.

Tempeh: It is a firm soybean product that can be used for grilling or stir-frying.

Edamame: Young soybeans that can be eaten as snacks after being steamed or added to different dishes when they are cooked this way.

3. Canned Beans

Low Sodium Options: To control salt intake, prefer low-sodium versions. These beans are protein and fibre rich which can be used in many dishes.

5. Dairy and Alternatives

1. Dairy Products
Greek Yogurt: It has high protein content but less sugar than normal yogurt. Go for the plain type to prevent added sugars.
Cottage Cheese: It can be eaten as a snack or included in recipes and is also a good source of protein and calcium.
Cheese: Chose hard cheeses such as cheddar, or parmesan that have low levels of lactose and sugar.

2. Dairy Alternatives

Almond Milk: Unsweetened varieties are low in carbohydrates and may replace milk in some cases.
Coconut Milk: Use unsweetened coconut milk to give a creamier texture to dishes.
Soy Milk: Unsweetened soy milk is another alternative with high protein content as compared to dairy milk.

Herbs, Spices, And Condiments

1. Herbs and Spices
Cinnamon: Used in baking, smoothies, oatmeal; known for blood sugar control.
Turmeric: Can be added to curries, soups, rice dishes; anti-inflammatory effects.
Garlic: fresh or powdered flavors without calories being added;
Basil, Oregano, Thyme, And Rosemary: Dried or fresh herbs with both taste and health benefits across various meals.

2. Condiments
Apple Cider Vinegar: Can be used in dressings and marinades to improve insulin sensitivity.
Mustard Is a condiment that adds taste without adding any calories through sugar into it
Hot Sauce Adds flavor without increasing calorie intake significantly containing minimal carbs per portion size of consumed spicy food items .
Soy Sauce : Low sodium versions help reduce salt intake .

6. Vegetables and Fruits

1. Canned and Frozen Vegetables
Non-Starchy Vegetables – green beans, spinach, broccoli cauliflower bell peppers should all be handy at home;

Tomatoes– canned tomatoes or tomato sauce without added sugars can be used in a variety of dishes.

2. Frozen Fruits
Berries: Blueberries, strawberries, raspberries, and blackberries can be consumed regularly since they have less sugar and are rich in antioxidants.
Avocado: Can be frozen as chunks for use in smoothies or thawed for salads/sandwiches.

Baking Essentials

1. Flours and Sweeteners
Almond Flour: A wheat flour alternative that is low in carbohydrates and great for baking.
Coconut Flour: Another low-carb flour option with a slightly sweet flavor.
Stevia Sweetener naturally zero calorie suitable for baking and drinks made from it
Monk Fruit Sweetener: A low carb substitute for sugar;

2. Leavening Agents
Baking powder/baking soda which has no carbs makes it possible to bake food items that will rise once they are baked.

Ready-to-Eat Snacks

1. Nuts and Seeds
Mixed Nuts – protein dense snack foods that also contain healthy fats,
Seed Mixes – These include pumpkin seeds, sunflower seeds and chia seeds making them highly nutritious snacks or ingredients for meals when mixed together;

2. Jerky
Beef Or Turkey Jerky – high protein snack that should be chosen from the store's shelves only if labeled as either low sodium or low-sugar/high-protein snack options with no preservatives added to it .

Breakfast Recipes

Your day needs a good breakfast to start with. A lot of emphasis should be given to this especially for diabetics. Planning your breakfast helps control the sugar levels in the body throughout the day hence helps you prevent morning cravings and maintain body energy. This section of the book contains numerous recipes that have been proven medically to manage diabetes

Air-Fried Veggie Frittata

Servings: 4
Time: 25 minutes
Nutritional Content (per serving):
Cal 150, Fat 10g, Protein 10g, Carbs 5g, Fibre 2g

Ingredients:
- 6 large eggs
- 60 milliliters (1/4 cup) of unsweetened almond milk
- 1 small onion, finely chopped
- 1 bell pepper, finely chopped
- 50 grams (1/2 cup) of shredded cheese
- 100 grams (1 cup) of chopped spinach
- 2 cloves garlic, minced
- Salt and black pepper, to taste
- Olive oil spray

Directions:
- Preheat the air fryer to 180°C (350°F).
- Put the almond milk, pepper, eggs, and salt in a bowl and whisk together.
- Stir in onion, bell pepper, cheese, spinach, and garlic.
- Spray an oven-safe dish with olive oil spray.
- Pour the egg mixture into the dish.
- Put the dish in the basket of the air fryer.
- Cook for 20-25 minutes, or until the frittata is golden.
- Allow to cool slightly before serving.

Almond Flour Pancakes

Servings: 4
Time: 20 minutes.
Nutritional Content (per serving):
Cal 210, Fat 15g, Protein 8g, Carbs 10g, Fibre 3g

Ingredients:
- 120 grams (1 cup) of almond flour
- 2 large eggs
- 60 milliliters (1/4 cup) of unsweetened almond milk
- 1 teaspoon baking powder
- 1 teaspoon vanilla extract
- 2 packets of stevia
- Olive oil spray

Directions:
- Preheat the air fryer to 180°C (350°F).
- In a bowl, mix almond flour, baking powder, and stevia.
- Get another bowl and whisk the almond milk, eggs, and vanilla extract together.
- Combine the wet and dry ingredients until smooth.
- Spray silicone muffin cups with olive oil spray.
- Divide the batter evenly among the cups.
- Place cups in the air fryer basket.
- Cook for 10-12 minutes until golden brown.
- Serve warm with sugar-free syrup.

Air-Fried Avocado Toast

Servings: 2
Time: 15 minutes.
Nutritional Content (per serving):
Cal 300, Fat 20g, Protein 6g, Carbs 22g, Fibre 10g

Ingredients:
- 2 slices of whole-grain bread
- 1 ripe avocado
- 1 small tomato, sliced
- 2 teaspoons of lemon juice
- Salt and black pepper, to taste
- Olive oil spray

Directions:
- Preheat the air fryer to 200°C (390°F).
- Spray bread slices with olive oil spray.
- Place in the air fryer and toast for 3–4 minutes until golden.
- Mix the pepper, lemon juice, salt, and avocado until you get a smooth mixture.
- Spread the avocado mixture on toasted bread.
- Top with tomato slices.
- Place again in the air fryer and allow to be for 2-3 minutes.
- Serve immediately.

Air-Fried Breakfast Sausage

Servings: 4
Time: 20 minutes.
Nutritional Content (per serving):
Cal 180, Fat 15g, Protein 10g, Carbs 1g, Fibre 0g

Ingredients:
- 450 grams (1 pound) of ground turkey
- 2 cloves garlic, minced
- 1 teaspoon dried sage
- 1 teaspoon dried thyme
- 1/2 teaspoon smoked paprika
- 1/2 teaspoon salt
- 1/4 teaspoon black pepper
- Olive oil spray

Directions:
- Preheat the air fryer to 200°C (390°F).
- In a bowl, combine ground turkey, garlic, sage, thyme, paprika, salt, and pepper.
- Form into 8 small patties.
- Spray patties with olive oil spray.
- Put the patties in the basket of the air fryer in a single layer.
- Cook for 10-12 minutes, flipping halfway through.
- Ensure the internal temperature reaches 74 °C (165 °F).
- Serve hot.

Air-Fried Greek Yogurt and Berry Parfait

Servings: 2
Time: 10 minutes.
Nutritional Content (per serving):
Cal 120, Fat 3g, Protein 12g, Carbs 12g, Fibre 2g

Ingredients:
- 240 grams (1 cup) of Greek yogurt
- 100 grams (1 cup) of mixed berries (strawberries, blueberries, raspberries)
- 15 grams (1 tablespoon) of chia seeds
- 1 teaspoon honey (optional)
- 1 teaspoon vanilla extract

Directions:
- In a bowl, mix Greek yogurt, chia seeds, honey, and vanilla extract.
- Layer the yogurt mixture and berries in serving glasses.
- Repeat layers until the glasses are filled.
- Top with a few extra berries.
- Chill for a few minutes before serving.

Air-Fried Omelette Muffins

Servings: 4
Time: 20 minutes.
Nutritional Content (per serving):
Cal 150, Fat 10g, Protein 12g, Carbs 3g, Fibre 1g

Ingredients:
- 6 large eggs
- 60 millilitres (1/4 cup) of unsweetened almond milk
- 1 small bell pepper, finely chopped
- 50 grams (1/2 cup) of shredded cheese
- 1 small onion, finely chopped
- 50 grams (1/2 cup) of chopped spinach
- Salt and black pepper, to taste
- Olive oil spray

Directions:
- Preheat the air fryer to 180°C (350°F).
- Put the pepper, eggs, salt, and almond milk in a bowl. Whisk the contents together.
- Stir in bell pepper, cheese, onion, and spinach.
- Spray silicone muffin cups with olive oil spray.
- Divide the egg mixture among the cups.
- Place cups in the air fryer basket.
- Cook for 12-15 minutes until set and golden.
- Allow to cool slightly before serving.

Air-Fried Tofu Scramble

Servings: 4
Time: 20 minutes.
Nutritional Content (per serving):
Cal 130, Fat 8g, Protein 10g, Carbs 5g, Fibre 2g

Ingredients:
- 450 grams (1 pound) of firm tofu, crumbled
- 1 small onion, finely chopped
- 1 bell pepper, finely chopped
- 1 small tomato, diced
- 1 teaspoon turmeric
- 1 teaspoon garlic powder
- 1 teaspoon onion powder
- Salt and black pepper, to taste
- Olive oil spray

Directions:
- Preheat the air fryer to 180°C (350°F).
- In a bowl, mix tofu, onion, bell pepper, tomato, turmeric, garlic powder, onion powder, salt, and pepper.
- Use an olive oil spray to spray the air fryer basket.
- Place the tofu mixture in the basket.
- Cook for 10-12 minutes, stirring halfway through.
- Serve warm.

Air-Fried Eggplant and Tomato Breakfast Bake

Servings: 4
Time: 30 minutes.
Nutritional Content (per serving):
Cal 140, Fat 7g, Protein 5g, Carbs 18g, Fibre 6g

Ingredients:
- 1 large eggplant, diced
- 2 large tomatoes, diced
- 1 small onion, finely chopped
- 2 cloves garlic, minced
- 30 millilitres (2 tablespoons) of olive oil
- 1 teaspoon dried oregano
- 1 teaspoon dried basil
- Salt and black pepper, to taste
- Olive oil spray

Directions:
- Preheat the air fryer to 200°C (390°F).
- In a bowl, mix eggplant, tomatoes, onion, garlic, olive oil, oregano, basil, salt, and pepper.
- Spray an oven-safe dish with olive oil spray.
- Place the vegetable mixture in the dish.
- Put the dish into the air fryer.
- Cook for 20-25 minutes, stirring occasionally, until vegetables are tender.
- Serve warm.

Air-Fried Spinach and Feta Breakfast Wrap

Servings: 4
Time: 15 minutes.
Nutritional Content (per serving):
Cal 200, Fat 11g, Protein 12g, Carbs 15g, Fibre 3g

Ingredients:
- 4 whole wheat tortillas
- 200 grams (1 cup) fresh spinach, chopped
- 100 grams (1/2 cup) feta cheese, crumbled
- 2 large eggs
- 1 small tomato, diced
- 2 cloves garlic, minced
- Salt and black pepper, to taste
- Olive oil spray

Directions:
- Preheat the air fryer to 180°C (350°F).
- Put the eggs, salt, and pepper in a bowl and whisk together.
- Spray a skillet with olive oil and scramble the eggs.
- Add spinach, tomato, and garlic to the skillet and cook until the spinach is wilted.
- Divide the mixture among the tortillas and sprinkle with feta cheese.
- Roll up each tortilla and place it in the air fryer basket.
- Cook for 3-5 minutes until the tortillas are crispy.
- Serve warm.

Air-Fried Cottage Cheese and Berry Bowl

Servings: 2
Time: 10 minutes.
Nutritional Content (per serving):
Cal 140, Fat 3g, Protein 14g, Carbs 16g, Fibre 4g

Ingredients:
- 240 grams (1 cup) of low-fat cottage cheese
- 100 grams (1 cup) of mixed berries (blueberries, strawberries, raspberries)
- 15 grams (1 tablespoon) of chia seeds
- 1 teaspoon honey (optional)
- 1 teaspoon vanilla extract

Directions:
- In a bowl, mix cottage cheese, chia seeds, honey, and vanilla extract.
- Divide the mixture into serving bowls.
- Top with mixed berries.
- Chill for a few minutes before serving.

Air-Fried Sweet Potato Hash

Servings: 4
Time: 20 minutes.
Nutritional Content (per serving):
Cal 180, Fat 7g, Protein 4g, Carbs 27g, Fibre 5g

Ingredients:
- 2 medium sweet potatoes, diced
- 1 small onion, finely chopped
- 1 bell pepper, finely chopped
- 2 cloves garlic, minced
- 30 millilitres (2 tablespoons) of olive oil
- 1 teaspoon smoked paprika
- Salt and black pepper, to taste
- Olive oil spray

Directions:
- Preheat the air fryer to 200°C (390°F).
- In a bowl, mix sweet potatoes, onion, bell pepper, garlic, olive oil, smoked paprika, salt, and pepper.
- Spray the basket of the fryer with olive oil spray.
- Place the sweet potato mixture in the basket.
- Cook for 20-25 minutes, shaking the basket halfway through.
- Serve warm.

Air-Fried Mushroom and Cheese Breakfast Bake

Servings: 4
Time: 25 minutes
Nutritional Content (per serving):
Cal 160, Fat 10g, Protein 12g, Carbs 5g, Fibre 2g

Ingredients:
- 200 grams (2 cups) mushrooms, sliced
- 1 small onion, finely chopped
- 2 cloves garlic, minced
- 100 grams (1/2 cup) shredded cheese
- 4 large eggs
- 60 millilitres (1/4 cup) of unsweetened almond milk
- Salt and black pepper, to taste
- Olive oil spray

Directions:
- Preheat the air fryer to 180°C (350°F).
- Put the almond milk, pepper, eggs, and salt in a bowl and whisk together.
- Stir in mushrooms, onion, garlic, and cheese.
- Spray an oven-safe dish with olive oil spray.
- Pour the egg mixture into the dish.
- Put the dish in the basket of the air fryer.
- Cook for 20-25 minutes, until set and golden.
- Allow to cool slightly before serving.

Air-Fried Zucchini and Egg Breakfast Boats

Servings: 4
Time: 20 minutes.
Nutritional Content (per serving):
Cal 110, Fat 7g, Protein 7g, Carbs 6g, Fibre 2g

Ingredients:
- 2 medium zucchinis, halved lengthwise
- 4 large eggs
- 1 small tomato, diced
- 1 small onion, finely chopped
- 1 teaspoon dried oregano
- Salt and black pepper, to taste
- Olive oil spray

Directions:
- Preheat the air fryer to 180°C (350°F).
- Scoop out the centers of the zucchinis to create boats.
- In a bowl, whisk together eggs, tomato, onion, oregano, salt, and pepper.
- Fill zucchini boats with the egg mixture.
- Spray a fryer basket with olive oil spray.
- Place the zucchini boats in the basket.
- Cook for 15-20 minutes until eggs are set.
- Serve warm.

Air-fried Cauliflower Breakfast Bites

Servings: 4
Time: 20 minutes.
Nutritional Content (per serving):
Cal 130, Fat 8g, Protein 7g, Carbs 10g, Fibre 4g

Ingredients:
- 1 medium head of cauliflower, grated
- 2 large eggs
- 50 grams (1/2 cup) of shredded cheese
- 1 small onion, finely chopped
- 2 cloves garlic, minced
- Salt and black pepper, to taste
- Olive oil spray

Directions:
- Preheat the air fryer to 200°C (390°F).
- In a bowl, mix grated cauliflower, eggs, cheese, onion, garlic, salt, and pepper.
- Form the mixture into small patties.
- Spray the air fryer basket with olive oil.
- Place patties in the basket.
- Cook for 10-12 minutes, flipping halfway through.
- Serve warm.

Air-Fried Breakfast Burrito

Servings: 4
Time: 15 minutes.
Nutritional Content (per serving):
Cal 250, Fat 12g, Protein 16g, Carbs 20g, Fibre 4g

Ingredients:
- 4 whole wheat tortillas
- 4 large eggs
- 100 grams (1/2 cup) of black beans, rinsed and drained
- 1 small bell pepper, finely chopped
- 50 grams (1/2 cup) of shredded cheese
- 1 small onion, finely chopped
- 1 teaspoon cumin
- Salt and black pepper, to taste
- Olive oil spray

Directions:
- Preheat the air fryer to 180°C (350°F).
- In a bowl, whisk eggs with salt, pepper, and cumin.
- Spray a skillet with olive oil and scramble the eggs.
- Add black beans, bell pepper, and onion to the skillet and cook until vegetables are tender.
- Divide the mixture among the tortillas and sprinkle with cheese.
- Roll up each tortilla and place it in the air fryer basket.
- Cook for 3-5 minutes until the tortillas are crispy.
- Serve warm.

Air-Fried Spinach and Mushroom Quiche

Servings: 4
Time: 25 minutes.
Nutritional Content (per serving):
Cal 180, Fat 12g, Protein 10g, Carbs 8g, Fibre 2g

Ingredients:
- 200 grams (2 cups) of chopped spinach
- 200 grams (2 cups) mushrooms, sliced
- 4 large eggs
- 60 millilitres (1/4 cup) of unsweetened almond milk
- 100 grams (1/2 cup) shredded cheese
- 1 small onion, finely chopped
- 2 cloves garlic, minced
- Salt and black pepper, to taste
- Olive oil spray

Directions:
- Preheat the air fryer to 180°C (350°F).
- Put the almond milk, pepper, eggs, and salt in a bowl and whisk together.
- Stir in spinach, mushrooms, cheese, onion, and garlic.
- Spray an oven-safe dish with olive oil spray.
- Pour the egg mixture into the dish.
- Put the dish in the basket of the air fryer.
- Cook for 20-25 minutes, until set and golden.

Air-Fried Broccoli and Cheddar Breakfast Cups

Servings: 4
Time: 20 minutes.
Nutritional Content (per serving):
Cal 160, Fat 10g, Protein 12g, Carbs 5g, Fibre 2g

Ingredients:
- 200 grams (2 cups) broccoli florets, chopped
- 4 large eggs
- 100 grams (1/2 cup) of shredded cheddar cheese
- 1 small onion, finely chopped
- 2 cloves garlic, minced
- Salt and black pepper, to taste
- Olive oil spray

Directions:
- Preheat the air fryer to 180°C (350°F).
- In a bowl, whisk together eggs, salt, and pepper.
- Stir in broccoli, cheddar cheese, onion, and garlic.
- Spray silicone muffin cups with olive oil spray.
- Divide the mixture among the cups.
- Place the cups in the air fryer basket.
- Cook for 12-15 minutes until set and golden.
- Allow to cool slightly before serving.

Air-Fried Apple Cinnamon Breakfast Bites

Servings: 4
Time: 15 minutes.
Nutritional Content (per serving):
Cal 120, Fat 5g, Protein 3g, Carbs 18g, Fibre 3g

Ingredients:
- 2 medium apples, diced
- 2 large eggs
- 60 grams (1/2 cup) of almond flour
- 2 teaspoons cinnamon
- 2 packets of stevia
- 1 teaspoon vanilla extract
- Olive oil spray

Directions:
- Preheat the air fryer to 180°C (350°F).
- In a bowl, mix apples, eggs, almond flour, cinnamon, stevia, and vanilla extract.
- Form the mixture into small balls.
- Spray the basket of the fryer with olive oil spray.
- Place balls in the basket.
- Cook for 10-12 minutes until golden brown.
- Serve warm.

Air-Fried Kale and Egg Breakfast Cups

Servings: 4
Time: 15 minutes.
Nutritional Content (per serving):
Cal 100, Fat 7g, Protein 6g, Carbs 4g, Fibre 1g

Ingredients:
- 100 grams (1 cup) kale, chopped
- 4 large eggs
- 1 small onion, finely chopped
- 1 small tomato, diced
- 1 teaspoon dried thyme
- Salt and black pepper, to taste
- Olive oil spray

Directions:
- Preheat the air fryer to 180°C (350°F).
- In a bowl, whisk eggs with salt, pepper, and thyme.
- Stir in kale, onion, and tomato.
- Spray silicone muffin cups with olive oil spray.
- Divide the mixture among the cups.
- Place the cups in the air fryer basket.
- Cook for 12-15 minutes until set and golden.
- Allow to cool slightly before serving.

Air-Fried Tomato and Basil Breakfast Tart

Servings: 4
Time: 20 minutes.
Nutritional Content (per serving):
Cal 140, Fat 9g, Protein 7g, Carbs 10g, Fibre 2g

Ingredients:
- 1 sheet of puff pastry
- 2 large eggs
- 100 grams (1/2 cup) of cherry tomatoes, halved
- 50 grams (1/2 cup) of shredded mozzarella cheese
- 1 teaspoon dried basil
- Salt and black pepper, to taste
- Olive oil spray

Directions:
- Preheat the air fryer to 180°C (350°F).
- Roll out the puff pastry and proceed to cut it into four squares.
- In a bowl, whisk eggs with salt, pepper, and basil.
- Stir in cherry tomatoes and cheese.
- Place a spoonful of the mixture onto each puff pastry square.
- Fold the corners of the pastry over the filling.
- Use an olive oil spray to spray the fryer basket.
- Place the tarts in the basket.
- Cook for 12-15 minutes until golden brown.
- Serve warm.

Lunch Recipes

Managing diabetes at lunchtime can be tough mainly because it demands finding the equilibrium between satisfying your hunger and sustaining constant blood sugar levels. The following air fryer lunch recipes are created specifically for this purpose. Being low in carbohydrates and sugar but high in fiber and proteins, these recipes will keep you feeling full and energized all day long. Whether you're home or making a packed meal for office, these recipes have delightful and handy options that help make living with your diabetes much easier as well as more fun.

Air-Fried Chicken Caesar Wrap

Servings: 4
Time: 20 minutes.
Nutritional Content (per serving):
Cal 320, Fat 15g, Protein 27g, Carbs 20g, Fibre 3g

Ingredients:
- 4 whole wheat tortillas
- 2 boneless, skinless chicken breasts
- 50 grams (1/2 cup) of grated Parmesan cheese
- 100 grams (1/2 cup) of Caesar dressing (low-fat)
- 100 grams (1 cup) romaine lettuce, chopped
- 1 small tomato, diced
- 1 teaspoon olive oil
- Salt and black pepper, to taste

Directions:
- Preheat the air fryer to 180°C (350°F).
- Season the chicken breasts using the olive oil, salt, and pepper.
- Place the chicken in the air fryer basket and cook for 10-12 minutes, flipping halfway through.
- Remove the chicken from the air fryer, let it cool slightly, then slice thinly.
- In a bowl, mix lettuce, tomato, Parmesan cheese, and Caesar dressing.
- Divide the salad mixture among the tortillas and top with sliced chicken.
- Roll up each tortilla and serve.

Air-Fried Shrimp Tacos

Servings: 4
Time: 15 minutes.
Nutritional Content (per serving):
Cal 210, Fat 10g, Protein 18g, Carbs 15g, Fibre 3g

Ingredients:
- 12 medium shrimp, peeled and deveined
- 4 corn tortillas
- 1 small avocado, sliced
- 100 grams (1 cup) of shredded cabbage
- 1 lime, cut into wedges
- 1 teaspoon olive oil
- 1 teaspoon chili powder
- Salt and black pepper, to taste
- Olive oil spray

Directions:
- Preheat the air fryer to 200°C (390°F).
- Put the shrimp, chili powder, pepper, salt, and olive oil in a bowl and toss to mix.
- Place shrimp in the air fryer basket and cook for 6–8 minutes, shaking halfway through.
- Warm tortillas in the air fryer for 2 minutes.
- Assemble tacos with shrimp, avocado, and cabbage.
- Serve with lime wedges.

Air-Fried Falafel wraps

Servings: 4
Time: 20 minutes.
Nutritional Content (per serving):
Cal 300, Fat 12g, Protein 10g, Carbs 38g, Fibre 10g

Ingredients:
- 1 can (400 grams) chickpeas, drained and rinsed
- 1 small onion, finely chopped
- 2 cloves garlic, minced
- 1 teaspoon ground cumin
- 1 teaspoon ground coriander
- 1/2 teaspoon baking powder
- 30 grams (1/4 cup) of flour
- Salt and black pepper, to taste
- 4 whole wheat tortillas
- 100 grams (1/2 cup) of hummus
- 100 grams (1 cup) of mixed greens
- Olive oil spray

Directions:
- Preheat the air fryer to 200°C (390°F).
- In a food processor, blend chickpeas, onion, garlic, cumin, coriander, baking powder, flour, salt, and pepper until smooth.
- Form the mixture into small patties.
- Spray the air basket in the air fryer with olive oil spray.
- Place patties in the basket and cook for 10-12 minutes, flipping halfway through.
- Spread hummus on tortillas and top with falafel patties and mixed greens.
- Roll up and serve.

Air-Fried Turkey and Avocado Sandwich

Servings: 4
Time: 10 minutes.
Nutritional Content (per serving):
Cal 250, Fat 12g, Protein 20g, Carbs 18g, Fibre 4g

Ingredients:
- 8 whole-grain breads
- 200 grams (7 ounces) of turkey breast, sliced
- 1 large avocado, sliced
- 4 slices of tomato
- 4 lettuce leaves
- 2 tablespoons light mayonnaise
- Salt and black pepper, to taste

Directions:
- Preheat the air fryer to 180°C (350°F).
- Spread mayonnaise on one side of each bread slice.
- Assemble sandwiches with turkey, avocado, tomato, and lettuce.
- Season with salt and pepper.
- Place sandwiches in the air fryer basket.
- Cook for 5-7 minutes, until bread is toasted.
- Serve immediately.

Air-Fried Veggie Quesadillas

Servings: 4
Time: 15 minutes.
Nutritional Content (per serving):
Cal 220, Fat 10g, Protein 10g, Carbs 25g, Fibre 4g

Ingredients:
- 4 whole wheat tortillas
- 100 grams (1 cup) of shredded cheese
- 1 small bell pepper, finely chopped
- 1 small onion, finely chopped
- 1 small zucchini, diced
- 1 teaspoon olive oil
- Salt and black pepper, to taste
- Olive oil spray

Directions:

- Preheat the air fryer to 180°C (350°F).
- In a skillet, heat olive oil and sauté bell pepper, onion, and zucchini until tender.
- Place a tortilla on a flat surface, sprinkle with cheese and sautéed veggies, then top with another tortilla.
- Spray the fryer basket with olive oil spray.
- Place the quesadilla in the basket and cook for 3-5 minutes, flipping halfway through.
- Cut into wedges and serve.

Air-Fried Chicken and Veggie Skewers

Servings: 4
Time: 20 minutes.
Nutritional Content (per serving):
Cal 240, Fat 8g, Protein 26g, Carbs 16g, Fibre 4g

Ingredients:
- 2 boneless, skinless chicken breasts, cubed
- 1 small bell pepper, cubed
- 1 small zucchini, sliced
- 1 small red onion, cubed
- 1 teaspoon olive oil
- 1 teaspoon dried oregano
- Salt and black pepper, to taste
- wooden skewers, soaked in water

Directions:
- Preheat the air fryer to 200°C (390°F).
- In a bowl, toss chicken and veggies with olive oil, oregano, salt, and pepper.
- Thread chicken and veggies onto skewers.
- Place skewers in the air fryer basket.
- Cook for 10-12 minutes, turning halfway through.
- Serve warm.

Air-Fried Salmon Patties

Servings: 4
Time: 15 minutes.
Nutritional Content (per serving):
Cal 200, Fat 10g, Protein 18g, Carbs 10g, Fibre 2g

Ingredients:
- 1 can (200 grams) salmon, drained and flaked
- 1 small onion, finely chopped
- 1 small bell pepper, finely chopped
- 1 large egg
- 30 grams (1/4 cup) of breadcrumbs
- 1 teaspoon Dijon mustard
- Salt and black pepper, to taste
- Olive oil spray

Directions:
- Preheat the air fryer to 200°C (390°F).
- In a bowl, mix salmon, onion, bell pepper, egg, bread crumbs, Dijon mustard, salt, and pepper.
- Form the mixture into small patties.
- Spray the air fryer basket with olive oil.
- Place patties in the basket.
- Cook for 8-10 minutes, flipping halfway through.
- Serve warm.

Air-Fried Veggie Spring Rolls

Servings: 4
Time: 15 minutes.
Nutritional Content (per serving):
Cal 150, Fat 5g, Protein 4g, Carbs 20g, Fibre 3g

Ingredients:
- 8 spring roll wrappers
- 1 small carrot, julienned
- 1 small cucumber, julienned
- 1 small bell pepper, julienned
- 50 grams (1/2 cup) of shredded cabbage
- 1 tablespoon soy sauce (low sodium)
- 1 teaspoon olive oil
- Olive oil spray

Directions:
- Preheat the air fryer to 200°C (390°F).
- In a bowl, mix carrot, cucumber, bell pepper, cabbage, soy sauce, and olive oil.
- Place a small amount of the veggie mixture on each spring roll wrapper and roll up tightly.
- Spray the air fryer basket with olive oil spray.
- Place spring rolls in the basket.
- Cook for 8-10 minutes, flipping halfway through.
- Serve with dipping sauce.

Air-Fried Chicken and Black Bean Tostadas

Servings: 4
Time: 15 minutes.
Nutritional Content (per serving):
Cal 260, Fat 12g, Protein 18g, Carbs 22g, Fibre 6g

Ingredients:
- 4 corn tortillas
- 200 grams (7 ounces) of cooked chicken breast, shredded
- 100 grams (1/2 cup) of black beans, drained and rinsed
- 50 grams (1/2 cup) of shredded cheese
- 1 small tomato, diced
- 1 small avocado, sliced
- 1 teaspoon cumin
- Salt and black pepper, to taste
- Olive oil spray

Directions:
- Preheat the air fryer to 200°C (390°F).
- In a bowl, mix chicken, black beans, cumin, salt, and pepper.
- Place the tortillas in the air fryer basket and cook for 3–4 minutes until crispy.
- Top tortillas with the chicken mixture and shredded cheese.
- Return to the air fryer and cook for 2-3 minutes until the cheese is melted.
- Top with tomato and avocado before serving.

Air-Fried Greek Chicken Wrap

Servings: 4
Time: 15 minutes.
Nutritional Content (per serving):
Cal 280, Fat 12g, Protein 22g, Carbs 20g, Fibre 3g

Ingredients:
- 4 whole wheat tortillas
- 2 boneless, skinless chicken breasts
- 50 grams (1/2 cup) feta cheese, crumbled
- 50 grams (1/2 cup) of diced cucumber
- 50 grams (1/2 cup) diced tomato
- 50 grams (1/4 cup) Greek yogurt (low-fat)
- 1 teaspoon dried oregano
- Salt and black pepper, to taste
- Olive oil spray

Directions:
- Preheat the air fryer to 180°C (350°F).
- Season chicken breasts with salt, pepper, and oregano.
- Place the chicken in the air fryer basket and cook for 10-12 minutes, flipping halfway through.
- Remove the chicken from the air fryer, let it cool slightly, then slice thinly.
- In a bowl, mix cucumber, tomato, feta cheese, and Greek yogurt.
- Divide the mixture among the tortillas and top with sliced chicken.
- Roll up each tortilla and serve.

Air-Fried Zucchini and Mushroom Panini

Servings: 4
Time: 10 minutes.
Nutritional Content (per serving):
Cal 230, Fat 10g, Protein 10g, Carbs 26g, Fibre 5g

Ingredients:
- 8 slices of whole-grain bread
- 100 grams (1 cup) of sliced zucchini
- 100 grams (1 cup) of sliced mushrooms
- 50 grams (1/2 cup) of shredded mozzarella cheese
- 1 tablespoon pesto
- Olive oil spray

Directions:
- Preheat the air fryer to 180°C (350°F).
- Begin by spreading the pesto on both sides of the bread slice.
- Assemble sandwiches with zucchini, mushrooms, and mozzarella cheese.
- Place sandwiches in the air fryer basket.
- Cook for 5-7 minutes, until bread is toasted and cheese is melted.
- Serve immediately.

Air-Fried Tuna and Avocado Salad

Servings: 4
Time: 10 minutes.
Nutritional Content (per serving):
Cal 180, Fat 10g, Protein 15g, Carbs 8g, Fibre 4g

Ingredients:
- 2 cans (200 grams) of tuna, drained and flaked
- 1 large avocado, diced
- 100 grams (1/2 cup) of cherry tomatoes, halved
- 1 small cucumber, diced
- 1 tablespoon olive oil
- 1 tablespoon lemon juice
- Salt and black pepper, to taste

Directions:
- In a bowl, mix tuna, avocado, cherry tomatoes, and cucumber.
- Drizzle with olive oil and lemon juice.
- Season with salt and pepper.
- Serve immediately.

Air-Fried Chickpea and Spinach Wrap

Servings: 4
Time: 15 minutes.
Nutritional Content (per serving):
Cal 260, Fat 10g, Protein 12g, Carbs 32g, Fibre 8g

Ingredients:
- 4 whole wheat tortillas
- 1 can (400 grams) chickpeas, drained and rinsed
- 100 grams (1 cup) of chopped spinach
- 1 small onion, finely chopped
- 1 small bell pepper, finely chopped
- 1 tablespoon olive oil
- 1 teaspoon ground cumin
- Salt and black pepper, to taste
- Olive oil spray

Directions:
- Preheat the air fryer to 180°C (350°F).
- In a skillet, heat olive oil and sauté onion and bell pepper until tender.
- Add chickpeas, spinach, cumin, salt, and pepper, and cook for another 5 minutes.
- Spread the mixture on tortillas and roll them up.
- Place the wraps in the air fryer basket.
- Cook for 3-5 minutes until crispy.
- Serve warm.

Air-Fried Caprese Sandwich

Servings: 4
Time: 10 minutes.
Nutritional Content (per serving):
Cal 200, Fat 10g, Protein 8g, Carbs 22g, Fibre 2g

Ingredients:
- 8 slices of whole-grain bread
- 200 grams (1 cup) of fresh mozzarella, sliced
- 1 large tomato, sliced
- 1 handful of fresh basil leaves
- 1 tablespoon balsamic glaze
- Olive oil spray

Directions:
- Preheat the air fryer to 180°C (350°F).
- Assemble sandwiches with mozzarella, tomato, and basil leaves.
- Drizzle with balsamic glaze.
- Place sandwiches in the air fryer basket.
- Cook for 5-7 minutes, until bread is toasted and cheese is melted.
- Serve immediately.

Air-Fried Veggie Burger

Servings: 4
Time: 15 minutes.
Nutritional Content (per serving):
Cal 220, Fat 8g, Protein 10g, Carbs 28g, Fibre 6g

Ingredients:
- 1 can (400 grams) of black beans, drained and rinsed
- 1 small onion, finely chopped
- 1 small bell pepper, finely chopped
- 1 small carrot, grated
- 1 large egg
- 30 grams (1/4 cup) of bread crumbs
- 1 teaspoon ground cumin
- Salt and black pepper, to taste
- Olive oil spray

Directions:
- Preheat the air fryer to 200°C (390°F).
- In a bowl, mash black beans and mix with onion, bell pepper, carrot, egg, bread crumbs, cumin, salt, and pepper.
- Form the mixture into patties.
- Spray the air fryer basket with olive oil spray.
- Place patties in the basket and cook for 8-10 minutes, flipping halfway through.
- Serve on whole grain buns with desired toppings.

Air-Fried Chicken and Veggie Wrap

Servings: 4
Time: 15 minutes.
Nutritional Content (per serving):
Cal 280, Fat 10g, Protein 22g, Carbs 28g, Fibre 4g

Ingredients:
- 4 whole wheat tortillas
- 2 boneless, skinless chicken breasts
- 1 small bell pepper, finely chopped
- 1 small zucchini, diced
- 1 small onion, finely chopped
- 1 teaspoon olive oil
- Salt and black pepper, to taste
- Olive oil spray

Directions:
- Preheat the air fryer to 180°C (350°F).
- Season chicken breasts with salt and pepper.
- Place the chicken in the air fryer basket and cook for 10-12 minutes, flipping halfway through.
- Remove the chicken from the air fryer, let it cool slightly, then slice thinly.
- In a skillet, heat olive oil and sauté bell pepper, zucchini, and onion until tender.
- Spread the veggie mixture and sliced chicken on tortillas.
- Roll up and serve.

Air-Fried Spinach and Feta Stuffed Peppers

Servings: 4
Time: 20 minutes.
Nutritional Content (per serving):
Cal 150, Fat 8g, Protein 10g, Carbs 10g, Fibre 3g

Ingredients:
- 2 large bell peppers, halved and seeded
- 100 grams (1 cup) of chopped spinach
- 100 grams (1/2 cup) feta cheese, crumbled
- 1 small onion, finely chopped
- 1 teaspoon dried oregano
- Salt and black pepper, to taste
- Olive oil spray

Directions:
- Preheat the air fryer to 180°C (350°F).
- In a bowl, mix spinach, feta cheese, onion, oregano, salt, and pepper.
- Fill bell pepper halves with the spinach mixture.
- Spray the air fryer basket with olive oil.
- Place bell peppers in the basket.
- Cook for about 20 minutes until the peppers are tender.
- Serve warm.

Air-Fried Chicken and Avocado Salad

Servings: 4
Time: 15 minutes.
Nutritional Content (per serving):
Cal 250, Fat 12g, Protein 20g, Carbs 14g, Fibre 5g

Ingredients:
- 2 boneless, skinless chicken breasts
- 1 large avocado, diced
- 100 grams (1 cup) of cherry tomatoes, halved
- 100 grams (1/2 cup) of corn kernels
- 1 small red onion, finely chopped
- 1 tablespoon olive oil
- 1 tablespoon lime juice
- Salt and black pepper, to taste

Directions:
- Preheat the air fryer to 180°C (350°F).
- Season chicken breasts with salt and pepper.
- Place the chicken in the air fryer basket and cook for 10-12 minutes, flipping halfway through.
- Remove the chicken from the air fryer, let it cool slightly, then dice.
- In a bowl, mix chicken, avocado, cherry tomatoes, corn, and red onion.
- Drizzle with olive oil and lime.

Air-Fried Eggplant Parmesan Sandwich

Servings: 4
Time: 20 minutes.
Nutritional Content (per serving):
Cal 230, Fat 9g, Protein 10g, Carbs 28g, Fibre 6g

Ingredients:
- 1 medium eggplant, sliced into rounds
- 30 grams (1/4 cup) of bread crumbs
- 30 grams (1/4 cup) of grated Parmesan cheese
- 1 large egg, beaten
- 8 slices of whole-grain bread
- 100 grams (1/2 cup) of marinara sauce
- 100 grams (1 cup) of shredded mozzarella cheese
- Olive oil spray

Directions:
- Preheat the air fryer to 200°C (390°F).
- Put the Parmesan cheese and bread crumbs in a bowl and mix.
- Dip eggplant slices in the beaten egg, then coat with the breadcrumb mixture.
- Spray the air fryer basket with olive oil.
- Place eggplant slices in the basket and cook for 8-10 minutes, flipping halfway through, until golden brown.
- Toast bread slices in the air fryer for 2-3 minutes.
- Assemble sandwiches by spreading marinara sauce on one side of each bread slice.
- Place eggplant slices on top, sprinkle with mozzarella cheese, and top with another slice of bread.
- Serve immediately.

Air-Fried Chickpea and Quinoa Salad

Servings: 4
Time: 15 minutes
Nutritional Content (per serving):
Cal 180, Fat 6g, Protein 8g, Carbs 24g, Fibre 6g

Ingredients:
- 1 can (400 grams) chickpeas, drained and rinsed
- 100 grams (1/2 cup) of cooked quinoa
- 100 grams (1/2 cup) of cherry tomatoes, halved
- 1 small cucumber, diced
- 1 small red onion, finely chopped
- 1 tablespoon of olive oil
- 1 tablespoon of lemon juice
- Salt and black pepper, to taste

Directions:
- In a bowl, mix chickpeas, quinoa, cherry tomatoes, cucumber, and red onion.
- Drizzle with olive oil and lemon juice.
- Season with salt and pepper.
- Serve immediately.

Dinner Recipes

Dinner is an important meal for maintaining balanced blood sugar levels, especially after a long day. The collection of dinner recipes below focuses on natural ingredients that provide a healthy, balanced meal without compromising on flavour. These air fryer recipes are tailored for diabetics, offering a variety of proteins, vegetables, and low-carb alternatives that are both nutritious and delicious. Whether you're preparing a quick weeknight meal or a more elaborate weekend dinner, these recipes will help you end your day on a healthy note.

Air-Fried Lemon Garlic Salmon

Servings: 4
Time: 20 minutes.
Nutritional Content (per serving):
Cal 300, Fat 18g, Protein 30g, Carbs 2g, Fibre 0g

Ingredients:
- 4 salmon fillets (150 grams or 6 ounces each)
- 2 tablespoons (30 millilitres) of lemon juice
- 2 cloves garlic, minced
- 1 tablespoon (15 millilitres) of olive oil
- 1 teaspoon dried oregano
- Salt and black pepper, to taste
- Olive oil spray

Directions:
- Preheat the air fryer to 180°C (350°F).
- In a small bowl, mix lemon juice, garlic, olive oil, oregano, salt, and pepper.
- Brush the salmon fillets with the lemon-garlic mixture.
- Spray the air fryer basket with olive oil.
- Place the salmon fillets in the basket and cook for 10-12 minutes, until cooked through.
- Serve immediately with a side of steamed vegetables.

Air-Fried Chicken and Broccoli Stir-Fry

Servings: 4
Time: 25 minutes
Nutritional Content (per serving):
Cal 250, Fat 10g, Protein 30g, Carbs 10g, Fibre 3g

Ingredients:
- 2 boneless, skinless chicken breasts, sliced into strips
- 200 grams (2 cups) of broccoli florets
- 1 small bell pepper, sliced
- 1 small onion, sliced
- 2 tablespoons (30 millilitres) of low-sodium soy sauce
- 1 tablespoon (15 millilitres) of olive oil
- 1 teaspoon garlic powder
- 1 teaspoon ground ginger
- Salt and black pepper, to taste
- Olive oil spray

Directions:
- Preheat the air fryer to 180°C (350°F).
- In a bowl, mix chicken strips with soy sauce, olive oil, garlic powder, ginger, salt, and pepper.
- Spray the air fryer basket with olive oil.
- Place the chicken in the basket and cook for 10 minutes.
- Add broccoli, bell pepper, and onion to the basket.
- Cook for another 10-12 minutes, shaking the basket halfway through.
- Serve immediately over brown rice or quinoa.

Air-Fried Shrimp Scampi

Servings: 4
Time: 15 minutes.
Nutritional Content (per serving):
Cal 220, Fat 12g, Protein 20g, Carbs 8g, Fibre 2g

Ingredients:
- 500 grams (1 pound) of large shrimp, peeled and deveined
- 2 tablespoons (30 millilitres) of lemon juice
- 2 cloves garlic, minced
- 1 tablespoon (15 millilitres) of olive oil
- 1 tablespoon (15 grams) of butter
- 1 teaspoon dried parsley
- Salt and black pepper, to taste
- Olive oil spray

Directions:
- Preheat the air fryer to 200°C (390°F).
- In a bowl, mix shrimp with lemon juice, garlic, olive oil, parsley, salt, and pepper.
- Spray the air fryer basket with olive oil.
- Place the shrimp in the basket and cook for 5-7 minutes, until pink and opaque.
- Put a small saucepan over low heat and melt some butter.
- Drizzle melted butter over cooked shrimp before serving.
- Serve immediately with a side of steamed vegetables or over whole-grain pasta.

Air-Fried Turkey Meatballs

Servings: 4
Time: 20 minutes.
Nutritional Content (per serving):
Cal 200, Fat 8g, Protein 25g, Carbs 8g, Fibre 2g

Ingredients:
- 500 grams (1 pound) of ground turkey
- 1 small onion, finely chopped
- 1 small bell pepper, finely chopped
- 1 large egg
- 30 grams (1/4 cup) of breadcrumbs
- 1 teaspoon dried oregano
- 1 teaspoon garlic powder
- Salt and black pepper, to taste
- Olive oil spray

Directions:
- Preheat the air fryer to 200°C (390°F).
- In a bowl, mix ground turkey, onion, bell pepper, egg, breadcrumbs, oregano, garlic powder, salt, and pepper.
- Form the mixture into meatballs.
- Spray the air fryer basket with olive oil.
- Place the meatballs in the basket and cook for 10-12 minutes, shaking the basket halfway through.
- Serve immediately with a side of marinara sauce and whole-grain pasta or zucchini noodles.

Air-Fried Stuffed Bell Peppers

Servings: 4
Time: 30 minutes.
Nutritional Content (per serving):
Cal 220, Fat 10g, Protein 15g, Carbs 20g, Fibre 5g

Ingredients:
- 4 large bell peppers, halved and seeded
- 200 grams (1 cup) of cooked quinoa
- 200 grams (1 cup) of black beans, drained and rinsed
- 100 grams (1/2 cup) of corn kernels
- 1 small onion, finely chopped
- 1 small tomato, diced
- 1 teaspoon ground cumin
- Salt and black pepper, to taste
- 50 grams (1/2 cup) of shredded cheese
- Olive oil spray

Directions:
- Preheat the air fryer to 180°C (350°F).
- In a bowl, mix quinoa, black beans, corn, onion, tomato, cumin, salt, and pepper.
- Fill bell pepper halves with the quinoa mixture.
- Spray the air fryer basket with olive oil.
- Place stuffed bell peppers in the basket and cook for 15-20 minutes, until the peppers are tender.
- Sprinkle shredded cheese over the stuffed peppers and cook for an additional 2-3 minutes, until the cheese is melted.
- Serve immediately.

Air-Fried Tofu Stir-Fry

Servings: 4
Time: 20 minutes
Nutritional Content (per serving):
Cal 220, Fat 12g, Protein 15g, Carbs 15g, Fibre 4g

Ingredients:
- 400 grams (14 ounces) of firm tofu, cubed
- 200 grams (2 cups) of broccoli florets
- 1 small bell pepper, sliced
- 1 small carrot, julienned
- 1 small onion, sliced
- 2 tablespoons (30 millilitres) of low-sodium soy sauce
- 1 tablespoon (15 millilitres) of sesame oil
- 1 teaspoon ground ginger
- Olive oil spray

Directions:
- Preheat the air fryer to 180°C (350°F).
- In a bowl, mix tofu cubes with soy sauce, sesame oil, and ground ginger.
- Spray the air fryer basket with olive oil.
- Place the tofu in the basket and cook for 10 minutes.
- Add broccoli, bell pepper, carrot, and onion to the basket.
- Cook for an extra 10 minutes while shaking the basket halfway through.
- Serve immediately over brown rice or quinoa.

Air-Fried Beef and Vegetable Skewers

Servings: 4
Time: 25 minutes
Nutritional Content (per serving):
Cal 300, Fat 15g, Protein 25g, Carbs 12g, Fibre 3g

Ingredients:
- 400 grams (14 ounces) of cubed beef sirloin
- 1 small zucchini, sliced
- 1 small bell pepper, sliced
- 1 small onion, quartered
- 8 cherry tomatoes
- 2 tablespoons (30 millilitres) of olive oil
- 1 tablespoon (15 millilitres) of balsamic vinegar
- 1 teaspoon dried rosemary
- Salt and black pepper, to taste
- wooden skewers, soaked in water

Directions:
- Preheat the air fryer to 200°C (390°F).
- In a bowl, mix olive oil, balsamic vinegar, rosemary, salt, and pepper.
- Thread beef, zucchini, bell pepper, onion, and cherry tomatoes onto the skewers.
- Brush with the olive oil mixture.
- Put the skewers in the fryer basket and allow to cook for about 15 minutes, turning halfway through.
- Serve immediately.

Air-Fried Chicken Parmesan

Servings: 4
Time: 25 minutes
Nutritional Content (per serving):
Cal 320, Fat 14g, Protein 35g, Carbs 14g, Fibre 3g

Ingredients:
- 4 boneless, skinless chicken breasts
- 1 large egg, beaten
- 50 grams (1/2 cup) of breadcrumbs
- 50 grams (1/2 cup) of grated Parmesan cheese
- 200 grams (1 cup) of marinara sauce
- 100 grams (1 cup) of shredded mozzarella cheese
- 1 teaspoon dried basil
- Salt and black pepper, to taste
- Olive oil spray

Directions:
- Preheat the air fryer to 200°C (390°F).
- In a bowl, mix breadcrumbs, Parmesan cheese, basil, salt, and pepper.
- Dip chicken breasts in the beaten egg, then coat with the bread crumb mixture.
- Spray the air fryer basket with olive oil.
- Place the chicken in the basket and cook for 10 minutes.
- Top the chicken breasts with marinara sauce and shredded mozzarella.
- Cook for an additional 5-7 minutes, until the cheese is melted and bubbly.

Air-Fried BBQ Pork Chops

Servings: 4
Time: 20 minutes.
Nutritional Content (per serving):
Cal 350, Fat 20g, Protein 30g, Carbs 10g, Fibre 1g

Ingredients:

- 4 pork chops (150 grams or 6 ounces each)
- 60 millilitres (1/4 cup) BBQ sauce (low sugar)
- 1 teaspoon smoked paprika
- 1 teaspoon garlic powder
- Salt and black pepper, to taste
- Olive oil spray

Directions:

- Preheat the air fryer to 200°C (390°F).
- In a bowl, mix BBQ sauce, smoked paprika, garlic powder, salt, and pepper.
- Brush pork chops with the BBQ sauce mixture.
- Spray the air fryer basket with olive oil.
- Place pork chops in the basket and cook for 12-15 minutes, flipping halfway through.
- Serve immediately with a side of steamed vegetables or a salad.

Air-Fried Vegetable Lasagna Rolls

Servings: 4
Time: 30 minutes.
Nutritional Content (per serving):
Cal 220, Fat 10g, Protein 15g, Carbs 20g, Fibre 4g

Ingredients:

- 8 lasagna noodles
- 200 grams (1 cup) of ricotta cheese
- 100 grams (1/2 cup) of shredded mozzarella cheese
- 1 small zucchini, diced
- 1 small carrot, grated
- 1 small bell pepper, diced
- 1 small onion, finely chopped
- 1 teaspoon dried basil
- 1 teaspoon garlic powder
- Salt and black pepper, to taste
- 200 grams (1 cup) of marinara sauce
- Olive oil spray

Directions:

- Preheat the air fryer to 180°C (350°F).
- Cook lasagna noodles according to package instructions and lay them flat on a baking sheet.
- In a bowl, mix ricotta cheese, zucchini, carrot, bell pepper, onion, basil, garlic powder, salt, and pepper.
- Spread the mixture evenly on each noodle and roll it up.
- Spray the air fryer basket with olive oil.
- Place lasagna rolls in the basket and cook for 15-20 minutes, until heated through.
- Top with marinara sauce and shredded mozzarella, then cook for an additional 2-3 minutes, until the cheese is melted.
- Serve immediately.

Air-Fried Cajun Shrimp and Vegetables

Servings: 4
Time: 20 minutes.
Nutritional Content (per serving):
Cal 230, Fat 10g, Protein 20g, Carbs 15g, Fibre 4g

Ingredients:
- 500 grams (1 pound) of large shrimp, peeled and deveined
- 1 small zucchini, sliced
- 1 small bell pepper, sliced
- 1 small red onion, sliced
- 1 small yellow squash, sliced
- 1 tablespoon (15 millilitres) of olive oil
- 1 teaspoon Cajun seasoning
- Salt and black pepper, to taste
- Olive oil spray

Directions:
- Preheat the air fryer to 200°C (390°F).
- In a bowl, mix shrimp and vegetables with olive oil, Cajun seasoning, salt, and pepper.
- Spray the air fryer basket with olive oil.
- Place shrimp and vegetables in the basket and cook for 10-12 minutes, shaking the basket halfway through.
- Serve immediately over brown rice or quinoa.

Air-Fried Stuffed Chicken Breasts

Servings: 4
Time: 30 minutes.
Nutritional Content (per serving):
Cal 280, Fat 12g, Protein 35g, Carbs 6g, Fibre 2g

Ingredients:
- 4 boneless, skinless chicken breasts
- 100 grams (1 cup) of chopped spinach
- 100 grams (1/2 cup) feta cheese, crumbled
- 1 small onion, finely chopped
- 1 teaspoon garlic powder
- Salt and black pepper, to taste
- Olive oil spray

Directions:
- Preheat the air fryer to 180°C (350°F).
- In a bowl, mix spinach, feta cheese, onion, garlic powder, salt, and pepper.
- Make a pocket in each chicken breast with a knife and stuff them with the spinach mixture.
- Spray the air fryer basket with olive oil.
- Place stuffed chicken breasts in the basket and cook for 20-25 minutes, until cooked through.
- Serve immediately.

Air-Fried Greek Chicken and Vegetables

Servings: 4
Time: 25 minutes
Nutritional Content (per serving):
Cal 250, Fat 12g, Protein 25g, Carbs 10g, Fibre 3g

Ingredients:
- 2 boneless, skinless chicken breasts, cubed
- 1 small zucchini, sliced
- 1 small bell pepper, sliced
- 1 small red onion, sliced
- 8 cherry tomatoes
- 2 tablespoons (30 millilitres) of olive oil
- 1 tablespoon (15 millilitres) of lemon juice
- 1 teaspoon dried oregano
- Salt and black pepper, to taste
- Olive oil spray

Directions:
- Preheat the air fryer to 200°C (390°F).
- In a bowl, mix chicken, vegetables, olive oil, lemon juice, oregano, salt, and pepper.
- Spray the air fryer basket with olive oil.
- Place the chicken and vegetables in the basket and cook for 12-15 minutes, shaking the basket halfway through.
- Serve immediately.

Air-Fried Teriyaki Salmon

Servings: 4
Time: 20 minutes.
Nutritional Content (per serving):
Cal 310, Fat 16g, Protein 30g, Carbs 8g, Fibre 0g

Ingredients:
- 4 salmon fillets (150 grams or 6 ounces each)
- 2 tablespoons (30 millilitres) of low-sodium teriyaki sauce
- 1 tablespoon (15 millilitres) of olive oil
- 1 teaspoon ground ginger
- 1 teaspoon garlic powder
- Salt and black pepper, to taste
- Olive oil spray

Directions:
- Preheat the air fryer to 180°C (350°F).
- In a small bowl, mix teriyaki sauce, olive oil, ginger, garlic powder, salt, and pepper.
- Brush salmon fillets with the teriyaki mixture.
- Spray the air fryer basket with olive oil.
- Place the salmon fillets in the basket and cook for 10-12 minutes, until cooked through.
- Serve immediately with a side of steamed vegetables.

Air-Fried Chicken Fajitas

Servings: 4
Time: 20 minutes.
Nutritional Content (per serving):
Cal 280, Fat 10g, Protein 30g, Carbs 20g, Fibre 4g

Ingredients:
- 2 boneless, skinless chicken breasts, sliced into strips
- 1 small bell pepper, sliced
- 1 small onion, sliced
- 1 tablespoon (15 millilitres) of olive oil
- 1 teaspoon chili powder
- 1 teaspoon ground cumin
- Salt and black pepper, to taste
- Olive oil spray
- 4 whole wheat tortillas

Directions:
- Preheat the air fryer to 200°C (390°F).
- In a bowl, mix chicken strips, bell pepper, onion, olive oil, chili powder, cumin, salt, and pepper.
- Spray the air fryer basket with olive oil.
- Place the chicken and vegetables in the basket and cook for 12-15 minutes, shaking the basket halfway through.
- Serve immediately with whole wheat tortillas.

Air-Fried Garlic Butter Shrimp

Servings: 4
Time: 15 minutes.
Nutritional Content (per serving):
Cal 220, Fat 14g, Protein 20g, Carbs 6g, Fibre 1g

Ingredients:
- 500 grams (1 pound) of large shrimp, peeled and deveined
- 2 cloves garlic, minced
- 2 tablespoons (30 grams) butter, melted
- 1 tablespoon (15 millilitres) of lemon juice
- 1 teaspoon dried parsley
- Salt and black pepper, to taste
- Olive oil spray

Directions:
- Preheat the air fryer to 200°C (390°F).
- In a bowl, mix shrimp with garlic, melted butter, lemon juice, parsley, salt, and pepper.
- Spray the air fryer basket with olive oil.
- Place the shrimp in the basket and cook for 5-7 minutes, until pink and opaque.
- Serve immediately with a side of steamed vegetables or over whole-grain pasta.

Air-Fried Eggplant Parmesan

Servings: 4
Time: 25 minutes
Nutritional Content (per serving):
Cal 240, Fat 12g, Protein 10g, Carbs 24g, Fibre 8g

Ingredients:
- 1 large eggplant, sliced into rounds
- 1 large egg, beaten
- 50 grams (1/2 cup) of breadcrumbs
- 50 grams (1/2 cup) of grated Parmesan cheese
- 200 grams (1 cup) of marinara sauce
- 100 grams (1 cup) of shredded mozzarella cheese
- 1 teaspoon dried basil
- Salt and black pepper, to taste
- Olive oil spray

Directions:
- Preheat the air fryer to 200°C (390°F).
- In a bowl, mix breadcrumbs, Parmesan cheese, basil, salt, and pepper.
- Dip eggplant slices in the beaten egg, then coat with the bread crumb mixture.
- Spray the air fryer basket with olive oil.
- Place eggplant slices in the basket and cook for 10 minutes.
- Top each slice with shredded mozzarella and marinara sauce.
- Cook for an additional 5-7 minutes, until the cheese is melted and bubbly.
- Serve immediately.

Air-Fried Lemon Herb Chicken Thighs

Servings: 4
Time: 25 minutes
Nutritional Content (per serving):
Cal 320, Fat 20g, Protein 30g, Carbs 2g, Fibre 0g

Ingredients:
- 4 chicken thighs (150 grams or 6 ounces each)
- 2 tablespoons (30 millilitres) of lemon juice
- 2 cloves garlic, minced
- 1 tablespoon (15 millilitres) of olive oil
- 1 teaspoon dried rosemary
- 1 teaspoon dried thyme
- Salt and black pepper, to taste
- Olive oil spray

Directions:
- Preheat the air fryer to 200°C (390°F).
- In a bowl, mix lemon juice, garlic, olive oil, rosemary, thyme, salt, and pepper.
- Use the lemon-herb mixture to coat the chicken thighs.
- Spray the air fryer basket with olive oil.
- Place chicken thighs in the basket and cook for 20-25 minutes, until cooked through.
- Serve immediately with a side of steamed vegetables or a salad.

Air-Fried Coconut Shrimp

Servings: 4
Time: 20 minutes.
Nutritional Content (per serving):
Cal 300, Fat 18g, Protein 20g, Carbs 15g, Fibre 5g

Ingredients:
- 500 grams (1 pound) of large shrimp, peeled and deveined
- 1 large egg, beaten
- 60 grams (1/2 cup) shredded coconut, unsweetened
- 60 grams (1/2 cup) of breadcrumbs
- 1 teaspoon paprika
- Salt and black pepper, to taste
- Olive oil spray

Directions:
- Preheat the air fryer to 200°C (390°F).
- In a bowl, mix shredded coconut, breadcrumbs, paprika, salt, and pepper.
- Dip shrimp in the beaten egg, then coat with the coconut mixture.
- Spray the air fryer basket with olive oil.
- Place the shrimp in the basket and cook for 10-12 minutes, until golden and crispy.
- Serve immediately with a side of dipping sauce or a salad.

Air-Fried Zucchini Boats

Servings: 4
Time: 25 minutes
Nutritional Content (per serving):
Cal 200, Fat 10g, Protein 15g, Carbs 15g, Fibre 4g

Ingredients:
- 4 medium zucchinis, halved and scooped out
- 200 grams (1 cup) of ground turkey
- 1 small onion, finely chopped
- 1 small bell pepper, diced
- 1 clove garlic, minced
- 1 teaspoon dried oregano
- 1 teaspoon garlic powder
- Salt and black pepper, to taste
- 100 grams (1 cup) of shredded mozzarella cheese
- Olive oil spray

Directions:
- Preheat the air fryer to 180°C (350°F).
- In a skillet, cook ground turkey with onion, bell pepper, garlic, oregano, garlic powder, salt, and pepper until browned.
- Fill the zucchini halves with the turkey mixture.
- Spray the air fryer basket with olive oil.
- Place the zucchini boats in the basket and cook for 15-20 minutes, until the zucchini is tender.
- Sprinkle shredded mozzarella over the zucchini boats and cook for an additional 2-3 minutes, until the cheese is melted.
- Serve immediately.

Snacks and Appetizers

One of the most common difficulties faced by many diabetics is finding healthy snacks and starters compatible with their diets. However, there should be no cause for alarm. This part provides various savory and healthy choices suitable for a munch in-between hours or at events. With an air fryer, it becomes simple to make these recipes within a short period while ensuring low carbohydrate and sugar content. Each morsel you take gives pleasure as well as serves your health purpose.

Air-Fried Zucchini Chips

Servings: 4
Time: 20 minutes
Nutritional Content (per serving):
Cal 110, Fat 7g, Protein 2g, Carbs 9g, Fibre 2g

Ingredients:
- 2 medium zucchinis, sliced thinly
- 2 tablespoons (30 millilitres) of olive oil
- 1 teaspoon garlic powder
- 1 teaspoon paprika
- Salt and black pepper, to taste
- Olive oil spray

Directions:
- Preheat the air fryer to 200°C (390°F).
- In a bowl, mix zucchini slices with olive oil, garlic powder, paprika, salt, and pepper.
- Spray the air fryer basket with olive oil.
- Place zucchini slices in the basket in a single layer.
- Cook for about 12 minutes while shaking the basket halfway through, until it becomes crispy.
- Serve immediately.

Air-Fried Cauliflower Bites

Servings: 4
Time: 25 minutes
Nutritional Content (per serving):
Cal 90, Fat 5g, Protein 3g, Carbs 8g, Fibre 3g

Ingredients:
- 1 medium cauliflower, cut into florets
- 2 tablespoons (30 millilitres) of olive oil
- 1 teaspoon smoked paprika
- 1 teaspoon garlic powder
- Salt and black pepper, to taste
- Olive oil spray

Directions:
- Preheat the air fryer to 200°C (390°F).
- In a bowl, mix cauliflower florets with olive oil, smoked paprika, garlic powder, salt, and pepper.
- Spray the air fryer basket with olive oil.
- Place cauliflower florets in the basket.
- Cook for 15-20 minutes, shaking the basket halfway through, until golden brown and crispy.
- Serve immediately with a dipping sauce.

Air-Fried Avocado Fries

Servings: 4
Time: 15 minutes.
Nutritional Content (per serving):
Cal 150, Fat 13g, Protein 2g, Carbs 9g, Fibre 5g

Ingredients:
- 2 ripe avocados, sliced
- 1 large egg, beaten
- 60 grams (1/2 cup) of breadcrumbs
- 1 teaspoon garlic powder
- 1 teaspoon paprika
- Salt and black pepper, to taste
- Olive oil spray

Directions:
- Preheat the air fryer to 200°C (390°F).
- In a bowl, mix breadcrumbs, garlic powder, paprika, salt, and pepper.
- Dip avocado slices in the beaten egg, then coat with the bread crumb mixture.
- Spray the air fryer basket with olive oil.
- Place avocado slices in the basket in a single layer.
- Cook for 10-12 minutes, until crispy and golden.
- Serve immediately with a dipping sauce.

Air-Fried Mozzarella Sticks

Servings: 4
Time: 20 minutes.
Nutritional Content (per serving):
Cal 180, Fat 11g, Protein 10g, Carbs 10g, Fibre 1g

Ingredients:
- 8 mozzarella sticks
- 1 large egg, beaten
- 60 grams (1/2 cup) of breadcrumbs
- 2 tablespoons (30 grams) grated Parmesan cheese
- 1 teaspoon dried oregano
- Salt and black pepper, to taste
- Olive oil spray

Directions:
- Preheat the air fryer to 200°C (390°F).
- In a bowl, mix breadcrumbs, Parmesan cheese, oregano, salt, and pepper.
- Dip mozzarella sticks in the beaten egg, then coat with the breadcrumb mixture.
- Spray the air fryer basket with olive oil.
- Arrange mozzarella sticks in the air fryer basket in a single layer.
- Cook for about 8 minutes, or until crispy and golden.
- Serve immediately with marinara sauce.

Air-Fried Sweet Potato Fries

Servings: 4
Time: 20 minutes
Nutritional Content (per serving):
Cal 160, Fat 7g, Protein 2g, Carbs 22g, Fibre 4g

Ingredients:
- 2 medium sweet potatoes, cut into fries
- 2 tablespoons (30 millilitres) of olive oil
- 1 teaspoon paprika
- 1 teaspoon garlic powder
- Salt and black pepper, to taste
- Olive oil spray

Directions:
- Preheat the air fryer to 200°C (390°F).
- In a bowl, mix sweet potato fries with olive oil, paprika, garlic powder, salt, and pepper.
- Spray the air fryer basket with olive oil.
- Place sweet potato fries in the basket in a single layer.
- Cook for about 20 minutes while shaking the basket halfway, until it becomes crispy and golden.
- Serve immediately.

Air-Fried Chicken Wings

Servings: 4
Time: 30 minutes.
Nutritional Content (per serving):
Cal 280, Fat 18g, Protein 24g, Carbs 4g, Fibre 1g

Ingredients:
- 1 kilogram (2 pounds) of chicken wings
- 2 tablespoons (30 millilitres) of olive oil
- 1 teaspoon garlic powder
- 1 teaspoon paprika
- 1 teaspoon cayenne pepper
- Salt and black pepper, to taste
- Olive oil spray

Directions:
- Preheat the air fryer to 200°C (390°F).
- In a bowl, mix chicken wings with olive oil, garlic powder, paprika, cayenne pepper, salt, and pepper.
- Spray the air fryer basket with olive oil.
- Place chicken wings in the basket in a single layer.
- Cook for 30 minutes, while shaking the basket halfway, or until it turns crispy and cooked through.
- Serve immediately with a dipping sauce.

Air-Fried Jalapeño Poppers

Servings: 4
Time: 20 minutes.
Nutritional Content (per serving):
Cal 130, Fat 10g, Protein 4g, Carbs 6g, Fibre 1g

Ingredients:

- 8 jalapeños, halved and seeded
- 100 grams (1/2 cup) of cream cheese
- 50 grams (1/2 cup) of shredded cheddar cheese
- 1 large egg, beaten
- 60 grams (1/2 cup) of breadcrumbs
- Salt and black pepper, to taste
- Olive oil spray

Directions:

- Preheat the air fryer to 200°C (390°F).
- In a bowl, mix cream cheese and cheddar cheese.
- Use the cheese mixture to stuff the jalapeño half.
- Dip stuffed jalapeños in beaten egg, then coat with breadcrumbs.
- Spray the air fryer basket with olive oil.
- Place jalapeños in the basket in a single layer.
- Cook for 10-12 minutes, until crispy and golden.
- Serve immediately.

Air-Fried Spinach and Feta Balls

Servings: 4
Time: 20 minutes.
Nutritional Content (per serving):
Cal 150, Fat 10g, Protein 6g, Carbs 10g, Fibre 2g

Ingredients:

- 200 grams (1 cup) of frozen spinach, thawed and drained
- 100 grams (1/2 cup) feta cheese, crumbled
- 1 large egg, beaten
- 60 grams (1/2 cup) of breadcrumbs
- 1 small onion, finely chopped
- 1 teaspoon garlic powder
- Salt and black pepper, to taste
- Olive oil spray

Directions:

- Preheat the air fryer to 200°C (390°F).
- In a bowl, mix spinach, feta cheese, egg, breadcrumbs, onion, garlic powder, salt, and pepper.
- Form the mixture into small balls.
- Spray the air fryer basket with olive oil.
- Place spinach balls in the basket in a single layer.
- Cook for 10-12 minutes, until crispy and golden.
- Serve immediately.

Air-Fried Stuffed Mushrooms

Servings: 4
Time: 20 minutes.
Nutritional Content (per serving):
Cal 120, Fat 8g, Protein 4g, Carbs 10g, Fibre 2g

Ingredients:
- 12 large mushrooms, stems removed
- 100 grams (1/2 cup) of cream cheese
- 50 grams (1/2 cup) of shredded cheddar cheese
- 1 small onion, finely chopped
- 1 teaspoon garlic powder
- 1 teaspoon dried parsley
- Salt and black pepper, to taste
- Olive oil spray

Directions:
- Preheat the air fryer to 180°C (350°F).
- In a bowl, mix cream cheese, cheddar cheese, onion, garlic powder, parsley, salt, and pepper.
- Stuff the mushroom cap using the cheese mixture.
- Spray the air fryer basket with olive oil.
- Place the stuffed mushrooms in the air fryer basket in a single layer.
- Cook for 12-15 minutes, until the mushrooms are tender and the tops are golden.
- Serve immediately.

Air-Fried Tofu Bites

Servings: 4
Time: 20 minutes.
Nutritional Content (per serving):
Cal 150, Fat 9g, Protein 12g, Carbs 8g, Fibre 2g

Ingredients:
- 400 grams (14 ounces) of firm tofu, drained and cubed
- 2 tablespoons (30 millilitres) of soy sauce
- 1 tablespoon (15 millilitres) of olive oil
- 1 teaspoon garlic powder
- 1 teaspoon smoked paprika
- Salt and black pepper, to taste
- Olive oil spray

Directions:
- Preheat the air fryer to 200°C (390°F).
- In a bowl, mix tofu cubes with soy sauce, olive oil, garlic powder, smoked paprika, salt, and pepper.
- Spray the air fryer basket with olive oil.
- Place tofu cubes in the basket in a single layer.
- Cook for 15-20 minutes, shaking the basket halfway through, until crispy.
- Serve immediately with a dipping sauce.

Air-Fried Falafel

Servings: 4
Time: 25 minutes
Nutritional Content (per serving):
Cal 200, Fat 10g, Protein 6g, Carbs 22g, Fibre 5g

Ingredients:

- 400 grams (1 can) chickpeas, drained and rinsed
- 1 small onion, chopped
- 2 cloves garlic, minced
- 30 grams (2 tablespoons) of fresh parsley, chopped
- 2 tablespoons (30 millilitres) of olive oil
- 1 teaspoon ground cumin
- 1 teaspoon ground coriander
- Salt and black pepper, to taste
- Olive oil spray

Directions:

- Preheat the air fryer to 200°C (390°F).
- In a food processor, combine chickpeas, onion, garlic, parsley, olive oil, cumin, coriander, salt, and pepper.
- Pulse until the mixture is thoroughly combined but still a little chunky.
- Make small balls or patties from the mixture.
- Spray the air fryer basket with olive oil.
- Place falafel in the basket in a single layer.
- Cook for 15 minutes, until crispy and golden.
- Serve immediately with a dipping sauce or in a pita.

Air-Fried Cheese and Broccoli Bites

Servings: 4
Time: 20 minutes.
Nutritional Content (per serving):
Cal 180, Fat 10g, Protein 8g, Carbs 14g, Fibre 2g

Ingredients:

- 200 grams (1 cup) broccoli florets, finely chopped
- 100 grams (1/2 cup) of shredded cheddar cheese
- 1 large egg, beaten
- 60 grams (1/2 cup) of bread crumbs
- 1 small onion, finely chopped
- 1 teaspoon garlic powder
- Salt and black pepper, to taste
- Olive oil spray

Directions:

- Preheat the air fryer to 200°C (390°F).
- In a bowl, mix broccoli, cheddar cheese, egg, bread crumbs, onion, garlic powder, salt, and pepper.
- Form the mixture into small balls.
- Spray the air fryer basket with olive oil.
- Place broccoli balls in the basket in a single layer.
- Cook for 10-12 minutes, until crispy and golden.

Air-Fried Coconut Chicken Bites

Servings: 4
Time: 20 minutes.
Nutritional Content (per serving):
Cal 230, Fat 13g, Protein 18g, Carbs 10g, Fibre 2g

Ingredients:
- 2 boneless, skinless chicken breasts, cut into bite-sized pieces
- 1 large egg, beaten
- 60 grams (1/2 cup) shredded coconut, unsweetened
- 60 grams (1/2 cup) of bread crumbs
- 1 teaspoon paprika
- Salt and black pepper, to taste
- Olive oil spray

Directions:
- Preheat the air fryer to 200°C (390°F).
- In a bowl, mix shredded coconut, bread crumbs, paprika, salt, and pepper.
- Dip chicken pieces in the beaten egg, then coat with the coconut mixture.
- Spray the air fryer basket with olive oil.
- Place chicken pieces in the basket in a single layer.
- Cook for 12-15 minutes, until crispy and golden.
- Serve immediately with a dipping sauce.

Air-Fried Garlic Parmesan Asparagus

Servings: 4
Time: 15 minutes.
Nutritional Content (per serving):
Cal 90, Fat 6g, Protein 4g, Carbs 6g, Fibre 3g

Ingredients:
- 1 bunch of asparagus, trimmed
- 2 tablespoons (30 millilitres) of olive oil
- 2 tablespoons (30 grams) grated Parmesan cheese
- 1 teaspoon garlic powder
- Salt and black pepper, to taste
- Olive oil spray

Directions:
- Preheat the air fryer to 200°C (390°F).
- In a bowl, mix asparagus with olive oil, Parmesan cheese, garlic powder, salt, and pepper.
- Spray the air fryer basket with olive oil.
- Place asparagus in the basket in a single layer.
- Cook for 10-12 minutes, shaking the basket halfway through, until tender and crispy.
- Serve immediately.

Air-Fried Eggplant Fries

Servings: 4
Time: 20 minutes.
Nutritional Content (per serving):
Cal 120, Fat 7g, Protein 2g, Carbs 12g, Fibre 4g

Ingredients:
- 1 large eggplant, cut into fries
- 2 tablespoons (30 millilitres) of olive oil
- 1 teaspoon garlic powder
- 1 teaspoon smoked paprika
- Salt and black pepper, to taste
- Olive oil spray

Directions:
- Preheat the air fryer to 200°C (390°F).
- In a bowl, mix eggplant fries with olive oil, garlic powder, smoked paprika, salt, and pepper.
- Spray the air fryer basket with olive oil.
- Place eggplant fries in the basket in a single layer.
- Cook for 20 minutes while shaking the basket halfway or until crispy and golden.
- Serve immediately.

Air-Fried Buffalo Cauliflower Bites

Servings: 4
Time: 25 minutes
Nutritional Content (per serving):
Cal 100, Fat 5g, Protein 2g, Carbs 12g, Fibre 4g

Ingredients:
- 1 medium cauliflower, cut into florets
- 2 tablespoons (30 millilitres) of hot sauce
- 2 tablespoons (30 millilitres) of olive oil
- 1 teaspoon garlic powder
- 1 teaspoon paprika
- Salt and black pepper, to taste
- Olive oil spray

Directions:
- Preheat the air fryer to 200°C (390°F).
- In a bowl, mix cauliflower florets with hot sauce, olive oil, garlic powder, paprika, salt, and pepper.
- Spray the air fryer basket with olive oil.
- Put the cauliflower florets in the air fryer basket in a single layer.
- Cook for 20 minutes, while shaking the basket halfway, or until crispy and golden.
- Serve immediately with a dipping sauce.

Air-Fried Chickpea Snacks

Servings: 4
Time: 20 minutes
Nutritional Content (per serving):
Cal 140, Fat 5g, Protein 6g, Carbs 18g, Fibre 6g

Ingredients:
- 400 grams (1 can) chickpeas, drained and rinsed
- 2 tablespoons (30 millilitres) of olive oil
- 1 teaspoon smoked paprika
- 1 teaspoon garlic powder
- Salt and black pepper, to taste
- Olive oil spray

Directions:
- Preheat the air fryer to 200°C (390°F).
- In a bowl, mix chickpeas with olive oil, smoked paprika, garlic powder, salt, and pepper.
- Spray the air fryer basket with olive oil.
- Place chickpeas in the basket in a single layer.
- Cook for 20 minutes, while shaking the basket halfway, or until crispy and golden.
- Serve immediately.

Air-Fried Portobello Mushroom Fries

Servings: 4
Time: 20 minutes
Nutritional Content (per serving):
Cal 120, Fat 7g, Protein 3g, Carbs 12g, Fibre 3g

Ingredients:
- 4 portobello mushrooms, sliced
- 2 tablespoons (30 millilitres) of olive oil
- 1 teaspoon garlic powder
- 1 teaspoon smoked paprika
- Salt and black pepper, to taste
- Olive oil spray

Directions:
- Preheat the air fryer to 200°C (390°F).
- In a bowl, mix mushroom slices with olive oil, garlic powder, smoked paprika, salt, and pepper.
- Spray the air fryer basket with olive oil.
- Place mushroom slices in the basket in a single layer.
- Cook for 20 minutes, while shaking the basket halfway, or until crispy and golden.
- Serve immediately.

Air-Fried Brussels Sprouts

Servings: 4
Time: 20 minutes
Nutritional Content (per serving):
Cal 110, Fat 7g, Protein 4g, Carbs 10g, Fibre 4g

Ingredients:
- 500 grams (1 pound) of Brussels sprouts, halved
- 2 tablespoons (30 milliliters) of olive oil
- 1 teaspoon garlic powder
- 1 teaspoon smoked paprika
- Salt and black pepper, to taste
- Olive oil spray

Directions:
- Preheat the air fryer to 200°C (390°F).
- In a bowl, mix Brussels sprouts with olive oil, garlic powder, smoked paprika, salt, and pepper.
- Spray the air fryer basket with olive oil.
- Place Brussels sprouts in the basket in a single layer.
- Cook for 20 minutes, shaking the basket halfway, or until it turns crispy and golden.
- Serve immediately.

Air-Fried Onion Rings

Servings: 4
Time: 20 minutes.
Nutritional Content (per serving):
Cal 150, Fat 8g, Protein 3g, Carbs 17g, Fibre 2g

Ingredients:
- 1 large onion, sliced into rings
- 1 large egg, beaten
- 60 grams (1/2 cup) of bread crumbs
- 1 teaspoon garlic powder
- 1 teaspoon paprika
- Salt and black pepper, to taste
- Olive oil spray

Directions:
- Preheat the air fryer to 200°C (390°F).
- In a bowl, mix bread crumbs, garlic powder, paprika, salt, and pepper.
- Dip onion rings in the beaten egg, then coat with the bread crumb mixture.
- Spray the air fryer basket with olive oil.
- Place onion rings in the basket in a single layer.
- Cook for 10-12 minutes, until crispy and golden.
- Serve immediately with a dipping sauce.

Dessert Recipes

Managing diabetes should not mean you avoid eating desserts. The air fryer dessert recipes below will enable you to eat sweet things with lower sugar content and carbohydrates therefore suitable for a diabetic. They are healthier than the traditional ingredients hence people can have their treats while still remaining healthy. Whether it is fruity delights or chocolatey indulgences, these are some of the best diabetic-friendly recipes that you may fall in love with.

Air-Fried Apple Cinnamon Rings

Servings: 4
Time: 20 minutes.
Nutritional Content (per serving):
Cal 120, Fat 4g, Protein 1g, Carbs 22g, Fibre 4g

Ingredients:
- 2 large apples, cored and sliced into rings
- 1 teaspoon ground cinnamon
- 1 tablespoon stevia
- 1 tablespoon (15 millilitres) of melted coconut oil
- Olive oil spray

Directions:
- Preheat the air fryer to 180°C (350°F).
- In a bowl, mix cinnamon and stevia.
- Brush apple rings with melted coconut oil and coat with a cinnamon-stevia mixture.
- Spray the air fryer basket with olive oil.
- Place apple rings in the basket in a single layer.
- Cook for 8-10 minutes, until tender and slightly crispy.
- Serve warm.

Air-Fried Banana Fritters

Servings: 4
Time: 15 minutes.
Nutritional Content (per serving):
Cal 140, Fat 5g, Protein 2g, Carbs 25g, Fibre 3g

Ingredients:
- 2 ripe bananas, mashed
- 60 grams (1/2 cup) of almond flour
- 1 teaspoon ground cinnamon
- 1 teaspoon vanilla extract
- 1 large egg, beaten
- Olive oil spray

Directions:
- Preheat the air fryer to 180°C (350°F).
- In a bowl, mix mashed bananas, almond flour, cinnamon, vanilla extract, and beaten egg.
- Form the mixture into small fritters.
- Spray the air fryer basket with olive oil.
- Place fritters in the basket in a single layer.
- Cook for 12 minutes, until golden and crispy.
- Serve warm.

Air-Fried Chocolate Avocado Brownies

Servings: 4
Time: 25 minutes
Nutritional Content (per serving):
Cal 180, Fat 12g, Protein 4g, Carbs 18g, Fibre 5g

Ingredients:
- 1 ripe avocado, mashed
- 2 large eggs, beaten
- 30 grams (1/4 cup) of unsweetened cocoa powder
- 60 grams (1/4 cup) of almond flour
- 2 tablespoons (30 millilitres) of coconut oil, melted
- 2 tablespoons stevia
- 1 teaspoon vanilla extract
- Olive oil spray

Directions:
- Preheat the air fryer to 180°C (350°F).
- In a bowl, mix mashed avocado, beaten eggs, cocoa powder, almond flour, melted coconut oil, stevia, and vanilla extract until smooth.
- Pour the mixture into a greased, air fryer-safe baking dish.
- Spray the air fryer basket with olive oil.
- Place the baking dish in the basket.
- Cook for 15–18 minutes, until set.
- Let cool before cutting into squares.

Air-Fried Cinnamon Sweet Potato Bites

Servings: 4
Time: 20 minutes.
Nutritional Content (per serving):
Cal 130, Fat 4g, Protein 2g, Carbs 24g, Fibre 4g

Ingredients:
- 2 medium sweet potatoes, peeled and cut into cubes
- 1 tablespoon olive oil
- 1 teaspoon ground cinnamon
- 1 tablespoon stevia
- Olive oil spray

Directions:
- Preheat the air fryer to 200°C (390°F).
- In a bowl, mix sweet potato cubes with olive oil, cinnamon, and stevia.
- Spray the air fryer basket with olive oil.
- Place sweet potato cubes in the basket in a single layer.
- Cook for 15–18 minutes, shaking the basket halfway through, until tender and crispy.
- Serve warm.

Air-Fried Berry Crumble

Servings: 4
Time: 25 minutes
Nutritional Content (per serving):
Cal 150, Fat 7g, Protein 2g, Carbs 20g, Fibre 4g

Ingredients:
- 200 grams (2 cups) of mixed berries
- 30 grams (1/4 cup) of almond flour
- 30 grams (1/4 cup) of rolled oats
- 2 tablespoons stevia
- 2 tablespoons (30 millilitres) of melted coconut oil
- 1 teaspoon ground cinnamon
- Olive oil spray

Directions:
- Preheat the air fryer to 180°C (350°F).
- In a bowl, mix almond flour, rolled oats, stevia, melted coconut oil, and cinnamon to form the crumble topping.
- Place the mixed berries in an air fryer-safe baking dish.
- Sprinkle the crumble topping over the berries.
- Spray the air fryer basket with olive oil.
- Place the baking dish in the basket.
- Cook for 15–18 minutes, until the topping is golden, and the berries are bubbling.
- Serve warm.

Air-Fried Peach Cobbler

Servings: 4
Time: 30 minutes.
Nutritional Content (per serving):
Cal 160, Fat 6g, Protein 3g, Carbs 24g, Fibre 3g

Ingredients:
- 3 medium peaches, sliced
- 30 grams (1/4 cup) of almond flour
- 30 grams (1/4 cup) of rolled oats
- 2 tablespoons stevia
- 2 tablespoons (30 millilitres) of melted coconut oil
- 1 teaspoon ground cinnamon
- Olive oil spray

Directions:
- Preheat the air fryer to 180°C (350°F).
- In a bowl, mix almond flour, rolled oats, stevia, melted coconut oil, and cinnamon to form the cobbler topping.
- Place peach slices in an air fryer-safe baking dish.
- Sprinkle the cobbler topping over the peaches.
- Spray the air fryer basket with olive oil.
- Place the baking dish in the basket.
- Cook for 20-25 minutes, until the topping is golden and the peaches are bubbling.
- Serve warm.

Air-Fried Blueberry Muffins

Servings: 4
Time: 20 minutes.
Nutritional Content (per serving):
Cal 150, Fat 8g, Protein 4g, Carbs 16g, Fibre 3g

Ingredients:
- 60 grams (1/2 cup) of almond flour
- 2 large eggs, beaten
- 1 teaspoon baking powder
- 2 tablespoons stevia
- 1 teaspoon vanilla extract
- 100 grams (1 cup) of fresh blueberries
- Olive oil spray

Directions:
- Preheat the air fryer to 180°C (350°F).
- In a bowl, mix almond flour, beaten eggs, baking powder, stevia, and vanilla extract until smooth.
- Fold in the fresh blueberries.
- Pour the batter into greased air fryer-safe muffin cups.
- Spray the air fryer basket with olive oil.
- Place the muffin cups in the basket.
- Cook for 15–18 minutes, until a toothpick inserted into the centre comes out clean.
- Let cool before serving.

Air-Fried Pineapple Rings

Servings: 4
Time: 15 minutes.
Nutritional Content (per serving):
Cal 100, Fat 1g, Protein 1g, Carbs 25g, Fibre 2g

Ingredients:
- 1 fresh pineapple, cored and sliced into rings
- 2 tablespoons (30 millilitres) of melted coconut oil
- 1 tablespoon stevia
- 1 teaspoon ground cinnamon
- Olive oil spray

Directions:
- Preheat the air fryer to 200°C (390°F).
- In a bowl, mix melted coconut oil, stevia, and cinnamon.
- Brush pineapple rings with the coconut oil mixture.
- Spray the air fryer basket with olive oil.
- Place pineapple rings in the basket in a single layer.

- Cook for 10-12 minutes, until caramelized and slightly crispy.
- Serve warm.

Air-Fried Chocolate Chip Cookies

Servings: 4
Time: 15 minutes.
Nutritional Content (per serving):
Cal 180, Fat 12g, Protein 3g, Carbs 18g, Fibre 3g

Ingredients:
- 60 grams (1/2 cup) of almond flour
- 2 tablespoons stevia
- 1 large egg, beaten
- 2 tablespoons (30 millilitres) of melted coconut oil
- 1 teaspoon vanilla extract
- 50 grams (1/4 cup) of sugar-free chocolate chips
- Olive oil spray

Directions:
- Preheat the air fryer to 180°C (350°F).
- In a bowl, mix almond flour, stevia, beaten egg, melted coconut oil, and vanilla extract until smooth.
- Fold in the sugar-free chocolate chips.
- Scoop tablespoons of dough and place them on a greased air fryer-safe baking sheet.
- Spray the air fryer basket with olive oil.
- Place the baking sheet in the basket.
- Cook for 10-12 minutes, until the edges are golden.
- Let cool before serving.

Air-Fried Stuffed Dates

Servings: 4
Time: 10 minutes.
Nutritional Content (per serving):
Cal 120, Fat 5g, Protein 2g, Carbs 18g, Fibre 3g

Ingredients:
- 16 large Medjool dates, pitted
- 60 grams (1/4 cup) of almond butter
- Olive oil spray

Directions:
- Preheat the air fryer to 180°C (350°F).
- Fill each date with almond butter.
- Spray the air fryer basket with olive oil.
- Place the stuffed dates in the basket in a single layer.
- Cook for 8-10 minutes, until the dates are warm and slightly crispy.
- Serve immediately.

Air-Fried Lemon Bars

Servings: 4
Time: 25 minutes.
Nutritional Content (per serving):
Cal 140, Fat 8g, Protein 3g, Carbs 14g, Fibre 2g

Ingredients:
- 60 grams (1/2 cup) of almond flour
- 2 large eggs, beaten
- 2 tablespoons stevia
- 1 tablespoon (15 millilitres) of lemon juice
- 1 teaspoon lemon zest
- 1 teaspoon vanilla extract
- Olive oil spray

Directions:
- Preheat the air fryer to 180°C (350°F).
- In a bowl, mix almond flour, beaten eggs, stevia, lemon juice, lemon zest, and vanilla extract until smooth.
- Pour the mixture into an already-greased air fryer-safe baking dish.
- Spray the air fryer basket with olive oil.
- Place the baking dish in the basket.
- Cook for 15–18 minutes, until set.
- Let cool before cutting into bars.

Air-Fried Raspberry Cheesecake Bites

Servings: 4
Time: 30 minutes.
Nutritional Content (per serving):
Cal 150, Fat 9g, Protein 4g, Carbs 14g, Fibre 2g

Ingredients:
- 200 grams (1 cup) of low-fat cream cheese
- 2 large eggs, beaten
- 2 tablespoons stevia
- 1 teaspoon vanilla extract
- 100 grams (1/2 cup) of fresh raspberries
- Olive oil spray

Directions:
- Preheat the air fryer to 160°C (320°F).
- In a bowl, mix cream cheese, beaten eggs, stevia, and vanilla extract until smooth.
- Fold in the fresh raspberries.
- Pour the mixture into greased air fryer-safe muffin cups.
- Spray the air fryer basket with olive oil.
- Place the muffin cups in the basket.
- Cook for 18-20 minutes, until set.
- Let cool before serving.

Air-Fried Coconut Macaroons

Servings: 4
Time: 15 minutes.
Nutritional Content (per serving):
Cal 130, Fat 9g, Protein 2g, Carbs 12g, Fibre 3g

Ingredients:
- 100 grams (1 cup) of unsweetened shredded coconut
- 2 large egg whites, beaten
- 2 tablespoons stevia
- 1 teaspoon vanilla extract
- Olive oil spray

Directions:
- Preheat the air fryer to 180°C (350°F).
- In a bowl, mix shredded coconut, beaten egg whites, stevia, and vanilla extract until well combined.
- Scoop tablespoons of the mixture and place them on a greased air fryer-safe baking sheet.
- Spray the air fryer basket with olive oil.
- Place the baking sheet in the basket.
- Cook for 10-12 minutes, until golden.
- Let cool before serving.

Air-Fried Pear Chips

Servings: 4
Time: 15 minutes.
Nutritional Content (per serving):
Cal 80, Fat 1g, Protein 1g, Carbs 20g, Fibre 4g

Ingredients:
- 2 medium pears, thinly sliced
- 1 tablespoon stevia
- 1 teaspoon ground cinnamon
- Olive oil spray

Directions:
- Preheat the air fryer to 160°C (320°F).
- In a bowl, mix pear slices with stevia and ground cinnamon.
- Spray the air fryer basket with olive oil.
- Place pear slices in the basket in a single layer.
- Cook for 15 minutes, shaking the basket halfway, until it turns crispy.
- Serve immediately.

Air-Fried Chocolate-Dipped Strawberries

Servings: 4
Time: 10 minutes.
Nutritional Content (per serving):
Cal 110, Fat 7g, Protein 1g, Carbs 10g, Fibre 2g

Ingredients:
- 200 grams (1 cup) of fresh strawberries
- 60 grams (1/2 cup) of sugar-free dark chocolate chips
- 1 tablespoon (15 millilitres) of coconut oil
- Olive oil spray

Directions:
- Preheat the air fryer to 160°C (320°F).
- In a microwave-safe bowl, melt the chocolate chips with coconut oil in 30-second intervals, stirring until smooth.
- Dip each strawberry into the melted chocolate, coating it evenly.
- Spray the air fryer basket with olive oil.
- Place the chocolate-dipped strawberries in the basket in a single layer.
- Cook for 5-7 minutes, until the chocolate is set.
- Let cool before serving.

Air-Fried Pumpkin Spice Donuts

Servings: 4
Time: 20 minutes.
Nutritional Content (per serving):
Cal 160, Fat 8g, Protein 4g, Carbs 18g, Fibre 4g

Ingredients:
- 60 grams (1/2 cup) of almond flour
- 2 tablespoons stevia
- 1 teaspoon pumpkin spice
- 2 large eggs, beaten
- 2 tablespoons (30 millilitres) of melted coconut oil
- 1 teaspoon vanilla extract
- Olive oil spray

Directions:
- Preheat the air fryer to 180°C (350°F).
- In a bowl, mix almond flour, stevia, pumpkin spice, beaten eggs, melted coconut oil, and vanilla extract until smooth.
- Pour the mixture into greased air fryer-safe donut g
- s.
- Spray the air fryer basket with olive oil.
- Place the donut moulds in the basket.
- Cook for 10-12 minutes, until a toothpick inserted into the centre comes out clean.
- Let cool before serving.

Air-Fried Chocolate Zucchini Bread

Servings: 4
Time: 25 minutes
Nutritional Content (per serving):
Cal 180, Fat 10g, Protein 4g, Carbs 20g, Fibre 4g

Ingredients:
- 60 grams (1/2 cup) of almond flour
- 1 medium zucchini, grated
- 2 large eggs, beaten
- 2 tablespoons stevia
- 2 tablespoons (30 millilitres) of melted coconut oil
- 1 tablespoon unsweetened cocoa powder
- 1 teaspoon vanilla extract
- 1 teaspoon baking powder
- Olive oil spray

Directions:
- Preheat the air fryer to 180°C (350°F).
- In a bowl, mix almond flour, grated zucchini, beaten eggs, stevia, melted coconut oil, cocoa powder, vanilla extract, and baking powder until well combined.
- Pour the mixture into a greased air fryer-safe loaf pan.
- Spray the air fryer basket with olive oil.
- Place the loaf pan in the basket.
- Cook for 20 minutes, or until a toothpick put into the centre comes out clean.
- Let it cool before slicing and serving.

Air-Fried Mango Coconut Balls

Servings: 4
Time: 15 minutes.
Nutritional Content (per serving):
Cal 120, Fat 6g, Protein 2g, Carbs 16g, Fibre 3g

Ingredients:
- 1 medium ripe mango, peeled and diced
- 100 grams (1 cup) of unsweetened shredded coconut
- 1 tablespoon stevia
- 2 tablespoons (30 millilitres) of melted coconut oil
- Olive oil spray

Directions:
- Preheat the air fryer to 180°C (350°F).
- In a blender, blend diced mango until smooth.
- In a bowl, mix mango puree, shredded coconut, stevia, and melted coconut oil until well combined.
- Scoop tablespoons of the mixture and form into balls.
- Spray the air fryer basket with olive oil.
- Place the mango coconut balls in the basket in a single layer.
- Cook for 8-10 minutes, until slightly crispy.

Air-Fried Churro Bites

Servings: 4
Time: 20 minutes.
Nutritional Content (per serving):
Cal 140, Fat 8g, Protein 2g, Carbs 15g, Fibre 2g

Ingredients:
- 60 grams (1/2 cup) of almond flour
- 2 large eggs, beaten
- 2 tablespoons stevia
- 1 teaspoon ground cinnamon
- 1 teaspoon vanilla extract
- 2 tablespoons (30 millilitres) of melted coconut oil
- Olive oil spray

Directions:
- Preheat the air fryer to 180°C (350°F).
- In a bowl, mix almond flour, beaten eggs, stevia, ground cinnamon, vanilla extract, and melted coconut oil until smooth.
- Pour the mixture into a greased air fryer-safe baking dish.
- Spray the air fryer basket with olive oil.
- Place the baking dish in the basket.
- Cook for 10-12 minutes, until set.
- Cut into bite-sized pieces and let cool before serving.

Air-Fried Apple Cinnamon Rolls

Servings: 4
Time: 20 minutes.
Nutritional Content (per serving):
Cal 170, Fat 7g, Protein 3g, Carbs 22g, Fibre 3g

Ingredients:
- 1 medium apple, peeled and finely chopped
- 60 grams (1/2 cup) of almond flour
- 2 tablespoons stevia
- 1 teaspoon ground cinnamon
- 2 large eggs, beaten
- 2 tablespoons (30 millilitres) of melted coconut oil
- 1 teaspoon vanilla extract
- Olive oil spray

Directions:
- Preheat the air fryer to 180°C (350°F).
- In a bowl, mix almond flour, stevia, ground cinnamon, beaten eggs, melted coconut oil, and vanilla extract until smooth.
- Fold in the chopped apple.
- Pour the mixture into greased air fryer-safe muffin cups.
- Spray the air fryer basket with olive oil.
- Place the muffin cups in the basket.
- Cook for 15–18 minutes, until a toothpick inserted into the centre comes out clean.
- Let cool before serving.

30 Days Meal Plan

To manage diabetes, you should pay attention to your diet and ensure that your meals are well-balanced, nutritious and suitable for blood sugar control. This 30-Day Meal Plan is aimed at making this process easier and it has a range of tasty healthy food recipes that can be conveniently cooked in an air fryer. Each day's menu has been carefully selected to include breakfast, lunch dinner, snacks and dessert that are low in carbs and sugar but outstandingly delicious as well as full of nutrients. In this meal plan, you will find different types of foods ranging from healthy breakfasts to satisfying lunches to delicious dinners and desserts. It also includes snacks and appetizers which can help keep your blood sugar levels stable in between meals. Diabetes-friendly diet with air-frying convenience as its centerpiece is what you get when following this schedule. It is a systematic program for managing diabetes effectively so as to ensure the individual gets a variety of good tasting nutritious meals daily. If you are new to using an air fryer or a seasoned pro, there is something for everyone in this meal plan thus enabling an easy way of achieving health eating though enjoyment thereof.

Day	Breakfast	Lunch	Dinner	Snack/Appetizer	Dessert
1	Spinach Feta Egg Bites	Chicken Caesar Salad Wrap	Lemon Herb Chicken	Zucchini Chips	Apple Cinnamon Mug Cake
2	Blueberry Almond Muffins	Turkey Lettuce Wrap	Garlic Butter Shrimp	Air-Fried Veggie Spring Rolls	Air-Fried Apple Cinnamon Rolls
3	Greek Yogurt & Berry Parfait	BBQ Chicken Flatbread	Air Fryer Salmon	Air-Fried Cauliflower Bites	Chocolate Avocado Mousse
4	Avocado Toast with Egg	Avocado Chicken Salad	Pork Tenderloin	Crispy Brussels Sprouts	Peanut Butter Banana Bites
5	Chia Seed Pudding	Caprese Salad	Stuffed Peppers	Garlic Parmesan Zucchini Fries	Mixed Berry Sorbet
6	Green Detox Smoothie	Asian Chicken Salad	Chicken Parmesan	Buffalo Cauliflower Bites	Air-Fried Peaches with Honey
7	Veggie Omelette	Tuna Salad Lettuce Wrap	Lemon Garlic Cod	Air-Fried Pickles	Cinnamon Spiced Apple Chips

8	Almond Flour Pancakes	Turkey Avocado Roll-Ups	Beef Stir-Fry	Mozzarella Sticks	Strawberry Greek Yogurt Bark
9	Berry Blast Smoothie	Greek Salad with Air-Fried Chickpeas	Air-Fried Tofu	Air-Fried Jalapeño Poppers	Raspberry Coconut Balls
10	Cottage Cheese & Fresh Fruit	Chicken Fajita Bowl	Balsamic Glazed Chicken	Sweet Potato Fries	Air-Fried Banana Chips
11	Spinach Mushroom Breakfast Quiche	Salmon Salad Lettuce Wrap	Herb Crusted Pork Chops	Avocado Fries	Lemon Poppy Seed Muffins
12	Pumpkin Spice Smoothie	Air-Fried Veggie Burger	Honey Mustard Chicken	Roasted Chickpeas	Chocolate Dipped Strawberries
13	Chocolate Almond Butter Smoothie	Quinoa Salad	Air-Fried Chicken Wings	Air-Fried Zucchini Slices	Mango Coconut Chia Pudding
14	Scrambled Eggs with Spinach	Shrimp Avocado Salad	Air Fryer Meatballs	Air-Fried Mushrooms	Air-Fried Pineapple
15	Peanut Butter Banana Smoothie	Air-Fried Fish Tacos	Air Fryer Steak	Broccoli Tots	Matcha Green Tea Smoothie
16	Apple Cinnamon Smoothie	Grilled Veggie Wrap	Stuffed Zucchini Boats	Spicy Sweet Potato Wedges	Spiced Pumpkin Smoothie
17	Air-Fried Tofu Scramble	Chicken Pesto Salad	Air Fryer Lamb Chops	Coconut Shrimp	Air-Fried Strawberries
18	Matcha Green Tea Smoothie	Cauliflower Rice Bowl	Air-Fried Pork Ribs	Air-Fried Green Beans	Blueberry Almond Smoothie

19	Kale Pineapple Smoothie	Air-Fried Chicken Caesar Salad	Air Fryer Mahi Mahi	Cauliflower Buffalo Wings	Chocolate Almond Energy Balls
20	Air-Fried Avocado Eggs	Avocado Quinoa Salad	Air Fryer BBQ Chicken	Air-Fried Parmesan Tomatoes	Orange Creamsicle Smoothie
21	Air-Fried Eggplant	Chicken Caprese Salad	Air-Fried Fish Fillets	Air-Fried Cheese Curds	Raspberry Chia Pudding
22	Air-Fried Apple Cinnamon Rolls	Turkey Bacon Lettuce Wrap	Air Fryer Stuffed Bell Peppers	Air-Fried Sweet Potato Bites	Beetroot Berry Smoothie
23	Spinach Feta Egg Bites	Greek Salad with Air-Fried Falafel	Air Fryer Lemon Pepper Wings	Crispy Green Beans	Pineapple Coconut Smoothie
24	Blueberry Almond Muffins	Chicken Avocado Bowl	Air Fryer Pork Tenderloin	Buffalo Tofu Bites	Air-Fried Caramelized Pears
25	Greek Yogurt & Berry Parfait	Avocado Tuna Salad	Air Fryer Garlic Shrimp	Air-Fried Radish Chips	Strawberry Kiwi Smoothie
26	Avocado Toast with Egg	Chicken Salad Stuffed Avocado	Air Fryer Beef Kebabs	Air-Fried Cauliflower	Air-Fried Honey Apples
27	Chia Seed Pudding	BBQ Tofu Bowl	Air Fryer Teriyaki Chicken	Crispy Chickpea Snacks	Cucumber Mint Smoothie
28	Green Detox Smoothie	Chicken Caesar Salad Wrap	Air Fryer Cajun Salmon	Air-Fried Broccoli	Air-Fried Cinnamon Apple Slices
29	Veggie Omelette	Caprese Salad	Air Fryer BBQ Ribs	Zucchini Chips	Air-Fried Pear Chips
30	Almond Flour Pancakes	Greek Salad	Air Fryer Herb Chicken	Air-Fried Brussels Sprouts	Air-Fried Banana Slices

Conclusion

Embarking on a journey to manage diabetes effectively through diet and lifestyle changes can be daunting, but it is an achievable and rewarding endeavour. This cookbook, "Diabetic Air Fryer Cookbook," aims to make this journey easier, more enjoyable, and sustainable. By incorporating over 100 healthy, delicious, low-carb, and low-sugar recipes tailored specifically for individuals with Type 1 and Type 2 diabetes, we hope to empower you to take control of your health and well-being. Throughout this book, we have explored the fundamentals of diabetes, the crucial role of diet in managing blood sugar levels, and the specific nutritional considerations necessary for diabetics. We delved into the benefits of air frying as a cooking method that reduces the need for excessive oil, thereby making meals healthier without compromising on taste and texture. We provided essential tips for getting started with your air fryer, including how to operate it, maintain it, and maximize its potential in your daily cooking routine. The recipe sections covered various meal categories, from breakfast to lunch, dinner, snacks, appetizers, and even desserts, ensuring that you have a comprehensive arsenal of diabetic-friendly meals at your disposal. The 30-Day Meal Plan offers a structured approach to help you integrate these recipes into your daily life, providing a balanced and varied diet that supports your health goals.

As we conclude this book, let us revisit some key takeaways and reflect on the broader implications of adopting a diabetic-friendly lifestyle.

Empowering Yourself with Knowledge
The first step to effectively managing diabetes is having adequate knowledge about it. Knowledge about the differences between Type 1 and Type 2 diabetes, the role of insulin, and the impact of carbohydrates on blood sugar levels is crucial. By educating yourself, you become more aware of how your body responds to different foods and lifestyle choices, allowing you to make informed decisions.

Remember that managing diabetes is not just about restricting certain foods but about creating a balanced and nutritious diet that supports overall health. Focus on incorporating a variety of whole foods, including lean proteins, healthy fats, fibre-rich vegetables, and low-glycaemic fruits. These choices help stabilize blood sugar levels and provide essential nutrients that support overall well-being.

The Role of Diet in Diabetes Management
Diet plays a central role in managing diabetes. The recipes in this book are designed to help you maintain stable blood sugar levels by focusing on low-carb, low-sugar ingredients. By avoiding refined sugars and opting for natural sweeteners like stevia or monk fruit, you can enjoy sweet treats without the adverse effects on your blood sugar.

Carbohydrate counting and portion control are essential skills for diabetics. Learning to read nutrition labels, measure portions accurately, and be mindful of serving sizes can prevent blood sugar spikes and help maintain a healthy weight. The recipes in this book provide detailed nutritional information to assist you in tracking your intake and making informed choices.

Customizing Recipes for Diabetic Needs

Adapting recipes to meet diabetic needs involves making simple substitutions and adjustments. For example, replacing high-carb ingredients with low-carb alternatives, using whole grains instead of refined grains, and incorporating more vegetables into dishes can make a significant difference. The recipes in this book are designed with these principles in mind, offering diabetic-friendly versions of classic favourites.

Portion control is another important aspect of managing diabetes. Serving sizes can have a direct impact on blood sugar levels, so it's essential to be mindful of how much you're consuming. The recipes in this book guide appropriate portion sizes, helping you stay within your dietary goals.

Building a Diabetic-Friendly Pantry

Stocking your pantry with diabetic-friendly ingredients makes meal preparation easier and more convenient. Focus on whole, unprocessed foods such as fresh vegetables, lean proteins, whole grains, and healthy fats. Keep a variety of herbs and spices on hand to enhance the flavor of your dishes without adding extra calories or carbs.

Low-carb flour, natural sweeteners, and high-Fibre foods are excellent staples for a diabetic-friendly pantry. These ingredients allow you to create delicious and nutritious meals that align with your dietary needs. Planning ahead and keeping your pantry well-stocked can help you stay on track and avoid unhealthy food choices.

Embracing a Healthy Lifestyle

While diet is a crucial component of diabetes management, it's also important to consider other aspects of a healthy lifestyle. Regular physical activity, adequate sleep, stress management, and regular medical check-ups all play a role in maintaining optimal health. Combining these elements with a balanced diet creates a holistic approach to managing diabetes.

Exercise helps regulate blood sugar levels, improve insulin sensitivity, and support overall cardiovascular health. Always do at least 150 minutes of moderate-intensity aerobic exercise per week, with strength training exercises. Consult with your healthcare provider before starting any new exercise program, especially if you have any complications related to diabetes.

Staying Motivated and Consistent

Maintaining a healthy lifestyle and managing diabetes require ongoing effort and commitment. The best way to stay motivated is to set realistic goals, monitor your progress, and celebrate your successes. Remember that it's okay to have occasional setbacks; the key is to get back on track and continue making healthy choices.

Support from family, friends, and healthcare professionals can also make a significant difference. Don't hesitate to reach out for help or join a support group where you can share experiences and learn from others. Having a strong support system can provide encouragement and accountability, making it easier to stick to your healthy habits.

Looking Ahead

As you continue your journey towards better health, remember that small, consistent changes can lead to significant improvements over time. The recipes and tips in this book are meant to be a starting point, inspiring you to explore new Flavors and cooking techniques that support your diabetic-friendly lifestyle.

Stay curious and open to trying new foods and recipes. The world of healthy cooking is vast and varied, offering endless possibilities for delicious and nutritious meals. By embracing this approach, you can enjoy a fulfilling and balanced diet that supports your health goals and enhances your quality of life.

In conclusion, managing diabetes through diet and lifestyle changes is a lifelong journey that requires dedication, knowledge, and support. This cookbook provides you with the tools and resources needed to create a diabetic-friendly diet that is both enjoyable and sustainable. With the help of an air fryer, you can prepare healthy, flavourful meals that fit seamlessly into your daily routine. We hope that this book has inspired you to take control of your health, experiment with new recipes, and discover the joy of cooking delicious, diabetic-friendly meals. Thank you for joining us on this journey, and we wish you all the best in your pursuit of a healthier, happier life.

Printed in Great Britain
by Amazon